WAYS OF KNOWING

Number 2 in the Series on Critical Information Organization in LIS,
Violet Fox and Kelsey George Sigle, Series Editors

WAYS OF KNOWING
ORAL HISTORIES ON THE WORLDS WORDS CREATE

Amanda Belantara and Emily Drabinski

Litwin Books
Sacramento, CA

Copyright 2025

Published in 2025 by Litwin Books

Litwin Books
PO Box 188784
Sacramento, CA 95822

http://libraryjuicepress.com/

This book is printed on acid-free paper.

All images in *Chicano Thesaurus* chapters courtesy of the Ethnic Studies Library, UC Berkeley.
All images in *Women's Thesaurus* chapters courtesy of Sarah Pritchard.
All images in *Homosaurus* chapters courtesy of the Homosaurus Editorial Board.

Publisher's Cataloging-in-Publication Data

Names: Belantara, Amanda, author. | Drabinski, Emily, author.
Title: Ways of knowing : oral histories on the worlds words create / Amanda Belantara and Emily Drabinski.
Description: Sacramento, CA : Litwin Books, 2025. | Series: Critical information organization in LIS ; 2. | Includes bibliographical references and index.
Identifiers: LCCN 2024941136 | ISBN 9781634001595 (acid-free paper)
Subjects: LCSH: Chicano Thesaurus – History. | Women's Thesaurus – History. | Homosaurus – History. | Subject headings – History. | Thesauri – History. | Librarians – Interviews.
Classification: LCC Z699.35.S92 B45 2024 | DDC 025.4--dc23
LC record available at https://lccn.loc.gov/2024941136

Contents

Introduction	1
The *Chicano Thesaurus*	9
Richard Chabrán on the *Chicano Thesaurus*	13
Lillian Castillo-Speed on the *Chicano Thesaurus*	49
The *Women's Thesaurus*	81
Mary Ellen Capek on the *Women's Thesaurus*	85
Sarah M. Pritchard on the *Women's Thesaurus*	121
The *Homosaurus*	155
K.J. Rawson on the *Homosaurus*	159
Adrian Williams on the *Homosaurus*	195
Bibliography	223
Acknowledgements	225
Index	229

Introduction

This book tells the stories behind alternative controlled vocabularies and the possibilities they create. The *Ways of Knowing Oral History Project* held at New York University Libraries currently contains six oral histories that document the creation of the *Chicano Thesaurus*, the *Women's Thesaurus*, and the *Homosaurus*. Though utilitarian in function, these alternative controlled vocabularies are not only about information access. The history of these three distinctive controlled vocabularies speaks to the power of collective action and community; of words and definitions and how they shape what can be searched, retrieved, and, ultimately, known. They reify worlds and ways of knowing that are often unknowable and unfindable by conventional library systems. These are stories of resistance, liberation, and the joys of self-determination.

We created the *Ways of Knowing Oral History Project* as two people personally impacted and compelled by the power dynamics of classification and description. As researchers, we are fascinated by socially constructed systems of order and control, how they become accepted as reality, and the material consequences they have on human lives. These systems are everywhere and dominate the flow of everyday life, reinforcing ideologies along the way. We must choose one bathroom and not another, tick one box and leave the rest blank, reifying binary gender categories and strictly bounded racial designations. These systems require our participation whether or not we've thought deeply about them or agree with the stories they tell us about who we are. Navigating and participating in the world depends on our compliance as we register for benefits, enroll a child in school, request a passport, and otherwise engage in everyday social life.

The systems used to organize and the terms used to describe library materials are examples of these fixed systems we find ourselves navigating. Library classification and cataloging structures shape how people search and retrieve materials; name people, places, things, and ideas; and research and think about the world. In these ways, knowledge organizing systems are worldmaking tools. They can solidify or subvert supposed norms. Every day, cataloging workers are required to use and contend with mainstream systems such as the Library of Congress' Classification and authorized Subject Headings. To optimize their search, library users must learn how to translate queries from their own language into the language of the catalog.

By forcing everything and everyone to fit into the confines of dominant normative structures, library catalogs imply that worlds outside of those norms don't exist. Words send messages. They send vibrations that play out in the brain and linger for generations, shaping how we understand the world in invisible ways. When libraries only rely on normative systems that dictate particular ways of being, knowing, or discovering the world, "those who do not fit in are neglected, silenced, delegitimized or simply considered exotic, religious, mythological: not real" (Querejazu, 2016). While some might think the words used to search for library materials are benign means to an end, they actually wield tremendous power; so much in fact that lawmakers have gone to court over them. Though out of public view, knowledge workers hold significant power. They can choose to intervene in these normative systems in order to make space for the rest of us (Belantara & Drabinski, 2022).

Recognizing these problems, cataloging and classification workers have long worked to revise and expand the Dewey Decimal System as well as the Library of Congress Classification (LCC) and Subject Headings (LCSH). Sanford Berman's landmark 1971 *Prejudices & Antipathies: A Tract on the LC Subject Heads Concerning People* put a stake in the ground for those organizing around the problem of universalized subject headings. While he was not the first or only person to address bias in descriptive vocabulary, this book introduced the problem of bias in cataloging to a broad and mainstream library audience. In a more recent example, librarians have suggested changes to the Library of Congress's Subject Authority Cooperative Program and joined together to enhance descriptions of material in African American history and culture, gender and sexuality studies, and other subjects. Institutions invest money and time into reparative cataloging projects that revise and change cataloging language to reflect changes in social and political understanding. These kinds of interventions have been well documented in library and information studies literature.

Rather than investigate projects that revise dominant structures, the *Ways of Knowing Oral History Project* documents instead what happens when communities come together to create new descriptive systems. We were interested in people and communities that require different tools to describe their worlds, leading us to explore counternarratives, ideas, and people that can only be (mis)represented in existing systems if they are subsumed by them. We wanted to know more about multiple ways of knowing and how the interventions of knowledge workers–catalogers and classifiers, librarians and archivists, students and activists–acknowledge and produce them. The oral histories included here demonstrate the concrete need for alternatives, not just to enable information discovery, but also as tools that challenge the imperialist ideas that are embedded in library catalogs. Alternative descriptive vocabularies can play an important part in upending systems and realities that have proclaimed themselves as the only way or truth.

Embracing alternative thesauri and the worlds they reflect and produce offers a different way forward than eliminating or attempting to correct normative systems. Rather than pursuing solutions that are bureaucratic, partial, and subject to government policies and confirmation, these efforts create something new that emerges from and belongs to the community itself. The projects documented here are revolutionary and joyful. Their creators do not wait for approval, and they do not answer to the Library of Congress. They do not ask for accommodation or inclusion. They document their own worlds, in their own words, with and for each other. If they didn't, no one else would. No one else really could. Building alternative thesauri is worldbuilding work. We use the word *worldbuilding* deliberately as a way of acknowledging the materiality of knowledge practices. They reflect and reproduce particular ways of being in the world through the iteration of language. Sending word lists back and forth through the mail builds a shared Chicano vocabulary and strengthens fundamental relationships between senders and receivers. Co-creating a controlled language also means building a world. When alternative vocabularies are placed next to terms from other worlds in the catalog, they can build bridges between them.

Each of these worlds exists alongside, enmeshed in, and counter to other worlds. Our informants inhabit normative worlds, as well as their own worlds, working as catalogers or administrators in university libraries, and as teaching faculty in multiple disciplines. The thesaurus terms also exist in the catalog alongside normative language. All three have been allocated unique source codes assigned by the Library of Congress that expand access to the vocabularies to other libraries who wish to include them in machine readable catalog records. When terms from multiple vocabularies sit alongside one another in a record, the catalog reveals multiple possible realities and can provide more nuanced metadata to represent the complex worlds humans inhabit.

The usage of alternative controlled thesauri moves the library catalog towards what anthropologists Mario Blaser and Marisol de la Cadena describe as the "uncommons." These scholars question the assumed meaning of common ground. Whose grounds are these? Who is welcome, and what is their relationship to each other? Who decides who belongs? Blaser and de la Cadena (2017) offer the uncommons as an alternative way of thinking about shared realities. The uncommons is "a condition that disrupts (yet does not replace) the idea of 'the world' as shared ground: an idea that appears as the condition of possibility for the common good and of commons" (p. 186). Such an idea mobilizes the catalog as a potential site of multiple meanings where difference does not need to be subordinated to the norm in order to be legible. Alternative vocabularies and knowledge organizing systems can help cultivate "the opportunity for a condition to emerge that… thrives on the encounter of heterogeneous worldings, taking place alongside each other with their divergent here(s) and now(s)" (2018, p. 16). To use the words of *Homosaurus* Editorial Board member K.J. Rawson, one purpose of alternative thesauri "is to make more words available... making things [worlds] legible and possible." Alternative vocabularies are powerful because they transform the stories that catalogs can tell and the worlds that are discoverable within them.

The three projects documented in this volume demonstrate what can happen when communities take control of their own description and categorization in the library and beyond. The transcripts that follow document these vocabularies through oral histories for the first time. *Ways of Knowing* is a primary source collection to support research and teaching about knowledge organization. We do not offer an analysis of the three systems as completed texts that represent some real or true way of organizing information. Indeed, we understand this work as always partial, contingent, and subject to change. So are people, places, and communities. Instead, we are interested in making legible the often-invisible processes of developing alternative descriptive and categorical systems. The oral histories document the wrestling and wrangling, the struggle and pleasure of groups of people coming together to develop tools that directly intervene in histories of exclusion, not by reforming existing systems, but by creating their own. We hear stories that are not documented in official reports or evident in the finished product. Chicano librarians send worksheets back and forth through the mail. Academic women's center staff rifle through file cabinets to find word lists. Queer librarians whisper "butt plug" and giggle together. We hear the grappling, the unavoidable challenge that comes with settling on a single term to describe human experience.

These oral histories remind listeners that controlled vocabulary projects are not just about word lists, they are about people. As Richard Chabrán shared, working on the *Chicano Thesaurus* and the *Chicano Periodical Index* "was really the establishment of a political identity, a group that worked together and struggled together on a lot of different things." In retelling a story about a poet who reads the *Women's Thesaurus* to find laughter and community amidst day-to-day misogyny, Mary

Ellen Capek brings to light the ways that alternative vocabularies can provide an important source of support, whether they are actually used to locate materials or not. These projects are about community and the worlds that are built when people come together to craft the terms that will ensure stories from their communities are findable and knowable into the future. Our hope is that this volume will inspire further interdisciplinary investigations about multiple epistemologies, social movement history, and the materiality of struggles for self-definition. The stories offer valuable insights for the field and the world as global communities recover, rebuild, and re-tell history from perspectives that have long been excluded from both historical and library catalog records.

This volume offers a vision of change. In each of the projects, whether institutionally-funded or not, authorized or rejected, we find people acting anyway. In some ways, the groups have been made stronger because they worked outside of systems that would not support them, finding ways to work independent of them. Autonomy and agency are key to their success as worlds are made on their own terms, not on the terms or conditions set by systems that have long excluded them. Perhaps the most powerful lesson we can take from these stories is that we can make our own worlds. We do not need to wait for permission and we cannot wait for someone else to act. We hope these narratives contribute to a shift in mindset that acknowledges the incommensurability of different ways of knowing. We do not dream of a common language, but of an uncommons where all languages can flourish. These projects each speak to a world in which no language is subordinate to any other, where none of us is asked to come to an agreement about a shared reality but instead can occupy and decide how our own is represented and understood.

Works Cited

Belantara, Amanda, and Emily Drabinski. "Working Knowledge: Catalogers and the Stories They Tell." *KULA: Knowledge Creation, Dissemination, and Preservation Studies* 6(3): 1-10. DOI: 10.18357/kula.233

Blaser, Mario, and Marisol de la Cadena. "The Uncommons: An Introduction." *Anthrolopologica* 59.2 (2017): 185-92. DOI: 10.3138/anth.59.2.t01

Cadena, Marisol de la, and Mario Blaser, eds. *A World of Many Worlds*. Durham: Duke University Press, 2018. DOI: 10.2307/j.ctv-125jpzq

Querejazu, Amaya. "Encountering the Pluriverse: Looking for Alternatives in Other Worlds." *Revista Brasileira de Política Internacional* 59 (November 16, 2016): e007. DOI: 10.1590/0034-7329201600207

The Chicano Thesaurus

Introduction

The story of the *Chicano Thesaurus* begins with the creation of the Chicano Studies Library at the University of California, Berkeley. In the late 1960s, student activists from marginalized communities formed the Third World Liberation Front and went on strike. They demanded that the university offer courses that included their own histories, histories that were often unavailable or unfindable within their library's collections. Students, activists, and academics partnered with library workers and even became library workers themselves in order to create and describe collections that would enable the study of histories that had been left out of the curriculum.

Students saw the creation of the Chicano Studies Library and its knowledge organizing systems as political actions. Their objective was not just to found and organize a library, but also to bring their community together to make concrete change. As student workers helped purchase materials and organize the new library's collection, they quickly realized that the existing library systems were inadequate for their library. Similarly, when seeking to create the first ever index of Chicana/o/x periodicals, they knew existing library vocabularies weren't going to work.

Richard Chabrán, the library's coordinator from 1975-1979, explained that the "terminology that was used [by the Library of Congress] in order to provide access was not what I would use, like a term like *Illegal aliens*. This is like them trying to socialize me; how I was going to call, look up and think about things that I did not think of in those terms. It was really objectionable to me to use those terms" (Chabrán, p.

6.) Chabrán and a network of librarians teamed up to create the *Chicano Thesaurus* out of recognition of the need for a new controlled vocabulary to provide subject access to the literature. They sought to apply for external funding in support of the *Chicano Periodical Index* project and the *Chicano Thesaurus*. However, the funding proposal had to be approved by and routed through the main university library administration, who refused to support a funding application that would go towards a project that didn't use Library of Congress Subject Headings.

Library staff didn't let that stop them. They were determined to create a thesaurus of their own. As Chicano Studies grew as a discipline across the United States and other libraries wanted access to the unique periodical collection they'd been developing at Berkeley, the staff were able to utilize the earnings from the sale of their microfilmed periodical collections to support the *Chicano Thesaurus* project. The Chicano Studies Library staff drafted a prospectus and got to work, collaborating with library workers developing Chicana/o/x collections in California, Arizona, and Texas, to form the Committee for the Development of Subject Access to Chicano Literatures.

Together, they published the first edition of the *Chicano Thesaurus*. The *Chicano Thesaurus* has gone through many technological changes and is now embedded in the Chicano Database, an electronic database of Chicano resources. The *Ways of Knowing Oral History Project* presents the history of the *Chicano Thesaurus* through the stories of two librarians who played key roles in its development and maintenance, Richard Chabrán and Lillian Castillo-Speed.

Chicano Thesaurus Timeline

1969 Library Founding
The La Raza Library was founded after funding was allocated following the Third World Liberation Front Strike.

1974 Chicano Classification System
Jose Antonio Arce completes and releases the Chicano Classification System.

1978 *Chicano Periodical Index* Project Begins
Led by Richard Chabrán, a group of fourteen librarians organized to index and provide subject access to eighteen key Chicana/o/x periodicals

1979 *Chicano Thesaurus* Published
The first edition of the *Chicano Thesaurus* is published.

1981 The *Chicano Periodical Index* is Published
The *Chicano Periodical Index*, the first index of Chicano periodicals, is published by GK Hall.

1990 The *Chicano Thesaurus* USMARC Code
The Library of Congress assigns the code "cht" to the *Chicano Thesaurus*, to be used in subfield 2 of 6XX MARC subject heading fields.

1990 The Chicano Database on CD-ROM
The Chicano Database is released on CD-ROM, the first ethnic studies database to be published in CD-ROM format.

2005 The *Chicano Thesaurus* Update
Lillian Castillo-Speed begins work with UCLA colleague Yolanda Retter Vargas to update the *Chicano Thesaurus*, adding sixty-five non-Chicana/o/x Latina/o/x terms and twenty-four LGBT terms at the time of the project's completion in 2007.

Richard Chabrán on the Chicano Thesaurus

Biography

Richard Chabrán received his primary and secondary education at St. Joseph School and Bishop Amat Memorial High School. Chabrán earned a bachelor's degree in anthropology and a master's in library and information studies at the University of California, Berkeley. He is a culture keeper, a promoter of digital technologies, and an educator in information studies. He served as the Coordinator of the Chicano Studies Library at UC Berkeley and the Coordinator of the Chicano Studies Center Research Library at UCLA.

Richard served as the founder and Director of the Center for Virtual Research in the College of Humanities, Arts, and Social Sciences at the University of California, Riverside where he developed the Community

Digital Initiative, which provided Internet access and training to Riverside's low-income community. He was a founder and policy advisor for the California Broadband Policy Network where he made numerous presentations before state level policy bodies. He has also served as a consultant and on advisory bodies for the Hispanic Division at the Library of Congress, the Educational Research Information Center, the National Library of Medicine Board of Regents and many more.

For twenty years Richard taught graduate students in the University of Arizona's School of Information where he played a leading role in the Knowledge River program. His publications include *The Chicano Periodical Index*, *Biblio-Política: Chicano perspectives on library service in the United States*, *The Latino Encyclopedia*, *Wired for Wireless: Towards Digital Inclusion and Next Generation Government-Led Wireless Networks* and many others. He is the recipient of numerous awards and is the team leader of the Latino Digital Archive Group.

About the Interview

The following transcribed interview of Richard Chabrán took place on August 11, 2022, as part of the *Ways of Knowing Oral History Project*. The interview was initially transcribed by using transcription software before being corrected by Belantara and Drabinski with input from Chabrán. Care was taken to avoid altering the original transcription's contents. However, the editors have formatted the following to improve readability and provided footnotes for clarity where appropriate. The oral history can be accessed through New York University Libraries.[1]

Transcript from the *Ways of Knowing Oral History Project*

Interviewee: Richard Chabrán, former coordinator of the Chicano Studies Library at the University of California, Berkeley and co-creator of the *Chicano Thesaurus*.

---

1. Richard Chabrán's oral history can be accessed through New York University Libraries. https://search.library.nyu.edu/permalink/01NYU_INST/1d6v258/alma990098389920107871.

Interviewers: Amanda Belantara & Emily Drabinski
Date: August 11, 2022
Location: Virtual Interview; Whittier College

Amanda Belantara: Today, we're interviewing Richard Chabrán, former coordinator of the Chicano Studies Library at University of California, Berkeley. The interview was conducted for the *Ways of Knowing Oral History Project*. The interview took place virtually on August 11th, 2022, recorded locally by Sonia Chaidez at Whittier College. The interviewers are Amanda Belantara and Emily Drabinski.

Emily Drabinski: Richard, can you tell us a bit about your background in education and what led you to librarianship?

Richard Chabrán: I went to Catholic school in a city called La Puente, California, which is a small town east of Los Angeles. I went to a parochial school called St. Joseph, and then to Bishop Amat High School. My brother was already attending the University of California Berkeley and he made sure to bring the papers home for me to apply. It was right after the Third World Strike.[2] There were a lot of demands to have an ethnic studies college and to have more minority professors and enroll more students of color. I was one of those students. I applied and I got in.

When I went to the university, I studied Anthropology. I have always been fascinated by culture and cultural transmission and how that happens. And I was also very motivated because I always felt that our history, as we are both Mexican and Puerto Rican, was not represented in my education. So, that led me to an interest in seeing how I could preserve that history, and I was really in Anthropology. But then, I got recruited to work in what was called the Chicano Studies Library at the University of California at Berkeley. It was a student library and student run, but it was always like an alternative library. One of the people in the library, his name was José Arce, he himself was a graduate student in Architecture, but he was the coordinator of the library at that time.

---
2. The Third World Liberation Front strike of 1969.

He said, "Hey, what are you doing?" and I explained that I was working as a museum preparator in the Lowie Museum of Anthropology.

And he said, "Why don't you come and work in the Chicano Studies Library?"

I said, "Okay, I'll go and do that."

So that was my entrance into working in the library. It wasn't my intention to become a librarian. I thought I would become an anthropologist. And when I first started working there, there had just been a report done on the status of the Chicano Studies Library. The University never did an assessment of what library resources would be available for the Ethnic Studies Department at that time. But the students said we need to have materials. It was really a struggle to try to make sure that we had the materials. So, they themselves started to collect materials.

My first job in the library, that was really important for me, was taking care of what was called the Serial Collection, which included newspapers, periodicals, and any kind of serial publication. There were publications that did not have regular publication schedules. At times even the numbering was not consistent. My job was to arrange and make sure they were saved. We saved them in vertical files. This was really important for me because I came to realize that those newspapers represented the voices of communities across the country that you don't often hear or read about. They were an education for me. And a little later, I took care of the journals.

A lot of the journals were alternative and were not indexed by major publishers nor the indexing services. Because I had to put them away, I became familiar with their content. When people would come into the library and say, "I want to know where this kind of article is," I was able to direct them to the articles they were looking for. I knew that with the growth of the literature…this was not sustainable. That was my entrance into my library career.

Many of the student workers had particular assignments. My assignment was to create a bibliography on folklore. My marching orders were to go out into all the different libraries at Berkeley, of which there were more than twenty, and find information about Chicano folklore. Looking back, that was a great way for me to learn about the libraries and to find them. What I found was that indeed there was material in all these different libraries about Chicanos. The problem was it was hidden, and I really felt that "the library" in quotations, did a very poor job of providing access to that material. That was an entrance into my library career.

Drabinski: It sounds like this is related to broader political struggles. So, could you tell us a little about what the political environment was like?

Chabrán: Just previous to the time I went to Berkeley, there was a Free Speech Movement.[3] And then there was the civil rights movement, and a Chicano student movement, and larger Chicano Movement. Richard Griswold del Castillo[4] says, "The Chicano Movement was a radical attempt to redefine the political, social, economic, and cultural status of millions of persons of Mexican descent."

It was partly motivated by the convergence of the anti-war movement, the civil rights movement and also the emergence of identity of this group of people. It was the first time they were starting to offer Chicano Studies courses. Initially it was called La Raza Studies.[5] At the same time, there were students that had advocated for the recruitment of more Mexican American students. When I arrived, there were few Chicanos on the campus.

---

3. The Free Speech Movement at the University of California, Berkely in fall of 1964. Additional information, and the UC Berkeley's Free Speech Movement Oral History Project, can be found at: https://www.lib.berkeley.edu/visit/bancroft/oral-history-center/projects/free-speech-movement.

4. Griswold del Castillo is an eminent scholar and professor emeritus of Chicana and Chicano Studies at San Diego State University.

5. Many discussions were held to determine the name of the La Raza program within the Ethnic Studies Department at the time of its founding. A course description from the fall 1969 La Raza Studies Bulletin provides the following description of La Raza: "The term "La Raza" (literally the race) is the most widespread term in usage among Spanish-speaking, Spanish-surname persons in the U.S...and refers mainly to those who are non-European "Americans." It is the race that came of three centuries of European rule over the natives of the Americas. The mestizo, the mixed-blood ones, are the mass of La Raza, but all Spanish speakers who do not identify with the conquering Europeans are of La Raza. Available through the Ethnic Studies Library at UC Berkeley: https://search.library.berkeley.edu/permalink/01UCS_BER/1ejhl6h/alma991005978339706532.

There were many other movements. There were the land grant struggles in New Mexico, the La Raza Unida political party that came about. There were farm worker struggles which manifested itself on our campus as an anti-lettuce campaign. There was a lot of pressure put on the university not to buy grapes. Those are the kind of struggles that were going on. Berkeley has this space that's called Sproul Plaza where people congregate. When you go to class, you would go past that space. There would always be a lot of speeches going on. Sometimes preachers would use this space to broadcast their message. The preachers were pretty famous. There was a lot going on during that time and I could not possibly capture it all.

Figure 1. The Third World Liberation Front Strike at the entrance to Sather Gate on the UC Berkeley campus.

Belantara: So, would you say that it was the environment that you were in at the time that really inspired you to then become a librarian when you weren't initially planning to do so?

Chabrán: I think that's a very fair statement. I've been reflecting about this more now and I think at the time one of the terms that caught my imagination was the idea of self-determination. Self-determination meant something different to different people.

To me, it was an opportunity to acknowledge that I had not learned the history of my people the way I thought it should be taught. Self-determination meant the opportunity to develop that history, and to develop those resources—so that not just my community, but the world would know it. That was a big inspiration for me. So yes, I wanted to become a librarian, but it was with a very particular purpose.

Belantara: What was the role of students in the founding of the collections and eventually the libraries?

Chabrán: We don't have a really perfect picture of that, but I would say that from my understanding, my knowledge, it was really students were the driving force, because they wanted a place where they could go and they could find material and where they could congregate, a place where they could have a safe place because there weren't very many Chicanos on the campus at that time.

They wanted to find out more about the issues that they were reading in the newspapers, the demonstrations they were at, the cultural festivals that they attended and the people that were creating this poetry that they heard—they wanted that material. I think that inspired them to start what we could call a reading room, which was a very small room in Dwinelle Hall. We had the collections and then we had this place where we could build these collections, but we really didn't have the money.

Belantara: Imagine that space that you just described, the reading room in Dwinelle Hall. Can you paint a picture for me?

Chabrán: You would go into this room and immediately there would be some kind of a desk that would be there to welcome people. Usually, it would be students that would be the ones that would be greeting people.

When you went in a little further, there would be on the right-hand side, there would be library shelving. But maybe library shelving is not the correct term. I would say it was more like the shelving that you might find in a professor's office. There were these little alcoves of books that were there.

On the other side, more to the back wall, there were vertical files. The vertical files held a lot of newspaper articles, or pamphlets, or flyers and all of that. A lot of things that we might consider ephemera. Those were the things that were really the most important part of this library. And on top of that, the library collected posters. The posters were a really important graphic part of what was going on out in the community. They were from the United Farm Workers from local artists. Many were from new artists. The walls were always filled with all these different kinds of posters and they covered different things like the war in Vietnam. And then, there was a catalog with the drawers with authors, titles and a shelf list, using a modified Library of Congress [Classification].

We weren't by ourselves. There were other universities where Latinos were engaged in building collections. For example, there were students at Stanford, San Diego, UCLA, Santa Barbara. We created an organization which we called ABC [La Asociación de Bibliotecas Chicanas] and we would meet periodically and try to help each other in what we were trying to do. It really helped fortify our voice and gave us a little bit of a platform.

I remember one time I was asked to go to San Jose, where they had a group that wanted to have a library, but they didn't have anything. They asked me, "Come over here. We're going to meet." Before I knew it, they were having a demonstration and I was in the library demonstrating, helping them. They got a section of the library. And today, that section is called the Africana, Asian American, Chicano, & Native American Studies Center (AAACNA). They're doing really great work. That's just to say that there was interest, primarily student-led, that started to really want to make a difference. We had the will to do this. We said, "We want to do it."

Belantara: All of these amazing materials that you were collecting for the Chicano Studies Collections, were they discoverable by the main library's catalog system at the time? Or would people need to visit the Chicano Studies Library in order to know that they were available?

Chabrán: They were not discoverable by the main library's catalog. One of the recommendations made in *Providing Library Services to the Chicano Studies Program*[6] report was to consider different models for collecting and making Chicano library material accessible. One model was to centralize everything. The second model was that there would be a bibliographic system that would make things discoverable in both places. The main library rejected both of those approaches. They said, "We don't have the money to do that. It would cost too much money."

While the Chicano Studies Library was concerned about the lack of the discoverability of their material in the main library, they didn't have any way of telling the main library, "You have to include what we have in your catalog." So, we would publish what we'd call the "Recent Additions to the Chicano Studies Library."[7] This was actually done by a few different libraries across the country; for example, at Austin and Santa Barbara. A few places would have these recent additions where they would find things and then they would put them there.

Now, that's not the same as having them discoverable in the main library. That didn't happen until much, much later. We were trying to do what we could to help at least the main library know what we were getting. But we also made this list of new additions available to more people across the country. The other thing we did was that we made some, what we would call subject bibliographies in certain areas like folklore, linguistics, and women that would reflect the findings of what we had found in the main library. So, we published those also as a way of saying what

---

6. Padilla, R. V. (1973). Providing Library Services for the Chicano Studies Program at the University of California, Berkeley: Policy Issues and Recommendations.

7. *Recent Additions to the Chicano Studies Library* was published by the Chicano Studies Library and was distributed nationally. *Recent Additions to the Chicano Studies Library*. Berkeley, Calif.: Chicano Studies Library, University of California. https://hdl.handle.net/2027/txu.059173018061575?urlappend=%3Bseq=3%3Bownerid=27021597768189411-7.

we knew was available in the branches of the main library. We were trying to do what we could to make things discoverable.

Belantara: What would you say were the benefits and then the disadvantages of being outside the main system?

Chabrán: The benefits were that *we* were going to do what we thought was the best. That meant collecting what we wanted to, organizing things the way we felt was more important, and starting to train people about how to use and to develop these systems. These were within our own purview. They couldn't stop us from doing that. I guess they could have, but they didn't.

Now the downside was that we didn't get money for doing the work. At that time, universities would provide a budget allocation to purchase material to cover library expenses in various disciplines. At Berkeley that money would go to the main library. The main library did not want to hear about sharing that money. A downside was we didn't get any of that money. On the other hand, one result of the Third World Strike, the Associated Student Body[8] developed a pot of money that could be used for exactly that purpose.

Belantara: So, student groups didn't just help start the collections and found the library. They actually supported it financially when the university wouldn't, is that correct?

Chabrán: Right. But it wasn't just the Chicano students. A vote was taken and the majority of all students supported this decision. During that time, students were pretty progressive. And, of course, there were Chicano students, men and women that were advocating for this at the time within student government. A disadvantage was that we weren't really part of what was happening on the inside of the University library.

Being on the inside we may have gotten certain benefits, but the library administration would've controlled what we could do. And we did

---

8. The Associated Students of the University of California (ASUC).

what we thought we should do with the resources we had. Judging from what happened at other places, this library became one of the most important collections in the country. At other universities they were part of the main library. Being on the inside might work for a while. However, in some places the support given to develop Chicano collections and services would go away once outside pressure subsided.

We were not against creating an interface with the main library. That interface came much later after other things happened. For example, many, many, many years later, there was Senate Concurrent Resolution 43,[9] which was where legislators said, "What's the University of California doing to support Latino studies?"

There was a task force of librarians that made several library recommendations. One recommendation was that the holdings of Chicano libraries in the University of California should be reflected in the university's online catalog. So now they are reflected. Not everything, but a lot of the monographic holdings are. Eventually, things got worked out after a lot of pressure. But it wasn't the idea of the library administration to do that. It was the pressure from outside. And it was not like, okay, we're just going to take and incorporate your material. You have to do it the way we're doing it. No, it was like we had a big impact on the way it was going to be incorporated.

Belantara: How did people working in the Chicano Collections view the library systems at that time?

Chabrán: Well, like I said, they viewed the library systems in the main library as inadequate. When the Chicano Studies Library first started, they tried to use the Dewey Decimal system, but it became very unwieldy with all the numbers. The numbers were going to start going across the book. That's when staff started to change to the Library of Congress system. But remember, at this time people were questioning, "How are we being described?"

---

9. California Senate Concurrent Resolution 43 (Presley, et al.), chaptered September 18, 1987. In 1987 the California State Legislature passed Concurrent Resolution 43. It called for the University of California to develop a Latino Agenda.

There was this utopian vision that we're going to make things different. Another issue was if you went into the main library, most of the books you'd find about Chicanos were in the E184 classification.[10] There was this kind of merging or melting together of all the materials. There was general dissatisfaction with the way that the materials were being classified and described. One of the consequences was that when they weren't in that E184 classification they were somewhere in those other twenty libraries. It was very difficult to really know where you would find something; take, for example, Chicano literature, which could either be with the Spanish literature or it could be with the English literature. And it was just very confusing for people.

So, José Arce created the Chicano Classification System. It's a modified Library of Congress Classification system. He added a PX classification for Chicano literature, not something separate that was inherited from a European system. And then there was literature within that classification system that was what we would call Chicanesca literature, which was literature that was written trying to emulate Chicano literature, but it was written by Anglos. The modified classification system had a place for that kind of literature. The modified system was something that was building off of what was coming out at the time. The Chicano Classification System didn't come about by Jose going to some room somewhere and just thinking, "Okay, this is the way it should be."

It was more like something that was developed from the bottom up based on the literature, based on what they were getting, and based on the experience of people that were putting it together. It was not some kind of academic thing. It was emergent. Also, the terminology that was used in order to provide access in the Library of Congress was not what I would use. For example, a term like *Illegal aliens*. This was an example of the library system trying to socialize me, how I was going to call and look up and think about the world. It was really objectionable to me to use those

---

10. The Library of Congress Classification class E184 designates "Elements in the population" and is used to classify materials related to various US populations "including racial, ethnic, and religious groups that have significance in the history of the United States." https://www.loc.gov/aba/publications/FreeLCC/LCC_E-F2023TEXT.pdf.

terms. And then there were cultural customs that we would have a certain name for and weren't very well represented by the English term that was used. It was linguistic, political, and cultural. All of those things didn't work for us.

I think the philosophy was we don't want to totally dismiss what the Library of Congress had to offer. It wasn't like we were trying to be oppositional, but we wanted to create new spaces where there were things that didn't fit in the traditional system. For example, I couldn't go to one place and find out where everything was. I had to go to these different places and figure out how each of them worked. It's not that it couldn't work, but it was not friendly. Just another example that I want to share with you is that on the Berkeley campus, there's the famous Bancroft Library that has a lot of collections about the history of California and Mexico. As a librarian, I was really good friends with a lot of historians. The historians would go and use that collection. And they would always kind of joke with me and say, "Well, we're not going to go and ask him for this material on Chicanos, because they wouldn't know what that was."

So just the language and the way it was represented, and if people didn't know about it. I mean, I'm not saying they were mean, they just didn't know. Because I saw this as a problem. I said, "I'm going to make a guide to all the archival collections that I think are relevant to people studying Mexican American history."

I started by making an appointment with the curator. I went over there and I told her what I was going to do and I gave her some examples and I said, "Can you help me? Because I really just want to work together."

And she says, "Well, I really can't help you. But there's this librarian that works in the Chicano Library across the way." Which is me, right?

So, she didn't know who I was and all that, but…and still she didn't take the opportunity for us to do something different. I think today things are different, but that was at that point. So, there were institutional barriers for us to do that kind of work. So, we did it by ourselves.

Drabinski: Now we'd like to talk a bit about the *Chicano Periodical Index*. Can you tell us about it and what the goal of that project was?

Chabrán: I continued to work on this Chicano serials project, which had these newspapers, journals and bulletins that we thought were really important and took a lot of space in the library. These publications were sought after because a lot of libraries didn't collect them. But then, within about five or six years, some libraries came to the realization of their importance and said, "We need them."

The professors at those places and Chicano Studies started saying, "We need to have those titles."

"The terminology that was used in order to provide access in the Library of Congress was not what I would use. For example, a term like Illegal aliens. *This was an example of the library system trying to socialize me, how I was going to call and look up and think about the world."*

And many libraries across the country didn't have them and some of them were not in print anymore. In order to preserve these publications, we had them microfilmed and made available through Bay Microfilms. We weren't looking to do this just for one library. We wanted to make these things available nationally. So, that was an important element to the larger goals we were trying to achieve.

Later on, when we developed the *Chicano Periodical Index*,[11] that was the next part of the project. Those of us that had worked in the library for a while knew how to find the material if somebody came in and said, "I want an article on women that focused on X, Y, and Z."

---

11. The *Chicano Periodical Index* was the first index of Chicano periodical literature. In 1978, the Chicano Periodical Indexing Project brought together a group of fourteen librarians across seven institutions. They indexed eighteen periodicals, among which were *Agenda, Atisbos, Aztlán, Caracol, Chicano Law Review, Con Safos, De Colores, Encuentro, El Grito, Grito del Sol, Journal of Mexican American History, Journal of Mexican American Studies* and *Somos.* https://search.library.berkeley.edu/permalink/01UCS_BER/iqob43/alma 991022 265479706532.

Several of us, because we had to keep answering these questions, knew it was there because we had put them on the shelves. It was the closeness, the proximity, of handling this material that allowed me to tell people where things were. I also knew that was not something that could be sustained. The literature was exploding. But, at that time there was no index. The material was there, but how do you get to it? We knew that we had to do something different. But many of these periodicals that became very important were not being indexed by the mainstream indexes. So, we thought wow, it's really important for us to create an index.

In late 1977, I'd been asked to talk to the Texas Library Association. And there was a group of Chicanos and Chicanas that said, "Can you come and talk about what you're doing?"

Soon after we got together and said, "We need to develop an index."

We didn't have any grants to do it, but we just saw a great need to do it. We said, "This is what we're going to do."

And we laid out a plan and we developed this prospectus for a *Chicano Periodical Index*. It was more like maybe more of a mission statement. So then, the goals of the index were to improve access to Chicano periodical literature, to provide a model index for developing a future comprehensive *Chicano Periodical Index* and database. And the specific objectives were to develop a vocabulary for indexing Chicano materials, to index eighteen journals and periodicals, and to publish and distribute that as an index. So that was really early, but we just said, "Oh, let's just do this, right?"

But we talked about it, and we had very specific goals.

Drabinski: Can you tell us a bit about who instigated the project and who was involved in this early iteration?

Chabrán: Well, I think that I instigated the project, I think that's fair to say. We developed this group, and we did a prospectus. And we had meetings where we had them at different library conferences. We said we wanted to index eighteen titles. But at that point we didn't say which titles they were. And so eventually, as a group, we agreed on which titles were going to be included. The principal people that were part of that effort were: Gilda Baeza, who was at El Paso Public Library; Rafaela Castro, who was a librarian at that time; Cesar Caballero, who was working with special collections at the University of Texas (now, he's the university librarian at Cal State San Bernardino); Luis Chaparro, who was at El Paso Community College; Elvira Chavarría, who was at the University of Texas at Austin; Karin Durán, who was at Cal State University Northridge; Robert McDowell, who was at Pan American University in Edinburg, Texas; Albert Milo, who is working at Fullerton Public Library; Helena Quintana, who was at New Mexico State; San Juanita Reyes, who was also at Pan American University; and Ron Rodriguez, who was working for me at UCLA.

These people made up the Committee for the Development of Subject Access to Chicano Literature. They were the indexers to the *Chicano Periodical Index*. I can tell you that for the bulk of the work that had to be done, these people did it. It would never have happened without them. It was so much work, so many titles. The index turned out to be four inches thick! It was a tremendous amount of work and they didn't get paid to do it. The indexers volunteered. They thought it was important. As I look back, that was a real commitment.

So, we had the interest of a lot of librarians that were willing to help us to do this. I think there was a lot of excitement, not just because of what we were doing, but because they were forming a network of librarians that ended up working on all kinds of different things. It was really the establishment of a political identity, a group that really worked together and struggled together on a lot of different things besides the index.

Drabinski: Can you tell us what kind of training people received? Did you have documentation to use?

Chabrán: We developed a *Chicano Periodical Index* Processing Manual. We distributed the manual and many of the indexers attended a national conference where we provided informal training. At the same time, we were working on this index of Chicano periodical literature; we understood that Chicano literature was beginning to be represented in mainstream databases like Dialog and BRS. While we were working on the index, we said we want people to understand how to access and search these other databases too. This was before a lot of people were being trained on online searching. Online searching was really expensive. It was different than it is now. Your search would be mediated through a librarian, and you had to sign up and the library got charged by the second.

Part of our job was familiarizing people with how this works. We wanted those librarians who were going to be indexers and were working with Latino populations to use many different tools that were being developed. So as part of that process, we got to see and be exposed to these different systems and subject headings and thesauri. Some of that made its way into our work.

I just want to emphasize that we didn't do this in isolation. We really were being informed by the things that were going on around us. We worked with this group called the National Chicano Research Network[12] to have a training where we brought people together to know how to use these systems. Once we had indexers, we had a different training session at Berkeley where the indexers came together, and we provided an overview of the processing manual. We went over the instructions for constructing the entries. Part of the processing manual described how the index terms would be used.

We created the thesaurus before we gave CHPI indexers the worksheets. They had the *Chicano Thesaurus* to help them select the subject headings. We assigned different periodicals to everybody. And then, what they did was, they sent those back to us, to me, and Francisco García helped a lot. And then they turned in their worksheets and we had them input into a system that was developed by this Vort Corporation using a minicomputer.

Some of the people that were indexers had never done that kind of work before. And so, there was a learning curve for them. We tried to provide as much orientation and instruction as we could. There were

---

12. The National Chicano Research Network was located at the University of Michigan's Institute of Social Research and provided support and training for Chicano scholars and students.

questions, but I think the steepest learning curve was working with a programmer. We had to learn all that technology and the different approaches. We had to agree to doing certain things versus other things. Francisco and myself did a lot of that interface with Vort Corporation. There was a tremendous learning curve and we learned a lot. When we got together, Francisco and I would go across the bay to Mountain View, which was about an hour and a half drive. The commute time was always a time of catching up. We did a lot of learning just through communicating with Tom Holt from the Vort Corporation.

Another catalyst for this work was when Betty Rose Rios invited me to be on the advisory board of ERIC[13] because I had a certain expertise. They had heard me speak at a regional conference. Betty Rose Rios was in charge of the ERIC Clearinghouse on Mexican Americans. She wanted to create a guide on how to use the ERIC database for Mexican Americans.

As part of the board, I ended up helping them to develop that guide. One of my motivations for becoming an advisory board member was to learn how to develop a bibliographic database. Betty introduced me to the people that were doing the work and their manual. I developed our own manual, which was modeled on the ERIC manual. The specifics were different, but we had something we could all follow.

We talked about this among the library staff where I was the coordinator at that time. Around 1976 I asked Linda Mariscal, one of the work study students I supervised, to develop a sample index. She developed a 3,000-item index using FAMULUS, a software program developed by the Department of Forestry, that allowed us to use the campus computer to develop various lists. So, we were just kind of getting our hands wet. By this time the main library had an online library catalog and databases, but all of this was very centralized.

At that point people weren't developing their own databases, and we wanted to have the freedom to do what we thought was important. That's why we went with an alternative tool. At the same time, we were working

---

13. ERIC (Educational Resources Information Center) is the U.S. Department of Education's database of resources related to education.

with people who were very sophisticated in their use of computers, and we just made it work for us. They didn't say, "This is the way it should be structured."

We worked on developing the database system together, so we became familiar with some of the technology that was emerging at that time that we had access to. We didn't have to ask the main library to please do this or let us use your system. We were able to just use that system to develop the index.

Belantara: So, once you assembled the initial index, how was it maintained and distributed?

Chabrán: Our main first objective was to develop an index, but we utilized software and hardware, looking forward to the time when the index would become an online database that could be searched. But our first goal was to get the print copy, so we did that. In that process, people would send their worksheets to Berkeley and then we would have them input by Vort. And then they'd get to see how it was coming together. Not all of us had access to that data, but the people at Berkeley and I had access using dumb terminals.[14]

It wasn't like the ones you have now. For example, there wasn't a graphics interface, just text. And so that's the way we did our initial editing. Indexers did all of this work. But really, in terms of the database, there was Francisco García Ayvens from UCLA and myself. We did a lot of that work. And we would actually spend a lot of time in Mountain View at the Vort Corporation. There were issues. Sometimes things weren't working. We worked together with the programmer and we did that maintenance work together. Then there was a question, how are we going to get the index out to the general public?

We talked to Norma Corral, a reference librarian from UCLA who said, "You might want to ask G.K. Hall because they've published all these catalogs from libraries and they published a catalog on Latin Amer-

---

14. A dumb terminal does not operate independently and depends on another computer in the network for processing.

ica that's really popular. So, you might want to ask if they would be interested in publishing it."

I approached G.K. Hall and they said, "Yes, we'll do it."

They published the first couple volumes of the *Chicano Periodical Index*. We had to get the data to them and then they made it look prettier though it still looked computer generated. G.K. Hall created an author title and subject index, and we added a list of the periodicals and the indexers, acknowledgements, and an essay. I think, for all of us, we were kind of like, "Wow, we did this."

And we were kind of a little surprised that we were able to do it. Like I said, that process really brought together this group of people and a lot of them still work together.

Belantara: Can you define what the *Chicano Thesaurus* is?

Chabrán: The *Chicano Thesaurus* is a collection of terms that allows people to describe the material that's about Chicanos and really, more broadly, about Latinos. But more specifically about Chicanos in ways that really reflect the literature. Because, up to that point, in the library that I was a coordinator of, we had abstained from really developing and systematically using a subject heading list. In other words, we wanted the subject headings to emerge from the literature that we were collecting and organizing and all that.

Belantara: Can you remember where and how the idea for the *Chicano Thesaurus* came about? Can you remember that moment and what the energy might have been like when that idea was first shared?

Chabrán: When we started thinking about doing the index, we knew that we had to have a controlled vocabulary. And so, for all of us, I don't know if I would describe it as excitement, but it was that this had to be done. It was more like, how are we going to do it? And the determination that it would be done.

This was really important because when the participating library collections first started to get developed, there was a little bit of competition between the different Chicano collections. Everybody wanted to have their own list. This was a watershed moment to say we're going to do something together. That was the excitement. We were not going to try to one up each other. We were going to do this together, whatever turned out.

It was really a way for us to come together and it was really empowering, let's say it that way. That we could work together, and we could actually do something. We started feeling like, wow, this is really possible. We can really do this. And so those people that were part of that initial group, we developed lifelong professional relationships and worked on a lot of different things, not just this. But we didn't lay out a detailed plan a year ahead of time, we just did it.

I don't want to give this appearance like there was this real well-planned thing and we followed all these different steps. We were just doing it. And sometimes I think it was great we did it and I wonder, "Would we have the guts to do that today?"

It was really emergent, that's the best term I can use, where we all were getting together. Nobody told us we had to do it. We did it voluntarily and it was something we just got together and we knew we had to do, what we had to do. And also, during that time, another person who was really influential was Sandy Berman.[15] His work on subject headings was inspirational. Later, I got to meet him and felt like telling him, "Hey, we're on the same page."

There were other people who were doing this kind of work, not specifically on Mexican Americans, but on other groups. The *Chicano Thesaurus* is really just a response to the need to describe material in ways which the people that it's about can understand, and that those terms and terminology would not be offensive—case in point, *Illegal aliens*.

---

15. Sanford Berman is a librarian and author well known for his 1979 work *Prejudices and Antipathies: A Tract on the LC Subject Heads Concerning People*, which brought wider attention to bias in Library of Congress Subject headings.

We always said, that was like a number one example, where the terms implied two things: that a person can be illegal, and that because you're a particular ethnicity that you are going to be illegal, right? So, there were all these negative associations with those terms like *Illegal aliens*. So, we wanted to have a terminology that was one that would be understood, and people would understand.

When I first started using the library, I would ponder where would catalogers put this? How would they describe us? Right?

The thesaurus was an attempt at describing ourselves. That was really important.

"I tried really hard to impress upon my students that if you want to make change, it's not just some bureaucratic thing. You have to be willing to hear, to listen, and to know that your own way of knowing is not the way everybody knows"

Belantara: Could you tell us about the Committee for the Development of Subject Access to Chicano Literature? How were members identified and selected?

Chabrán: We had met people. We had these meetings and conferences. Based on that ABC group,[16] that was the beginning of some of them. But that was mostly California. And then through the American Library Association conferences, and regional conferences like the Texas Library Association or the New Mexico Library Association; we were starting to meet at those places. The committee was built on those connections. Then we would ask, "Okay, who are we missing? Who else is doing this work?"

---

16. La Asociacion de Bibliotecas Chicanas (ABC) was a group of library workers who shared interests in the growth and development of Chicano libraries.

And so then there were a few other people that really weren't part of our initial conversation that came about. We reached out to them, and they were very interested in doing this. That's the way we did it. It was not a systematic search. It was really the people that we were meeting with informally at these conferences that we brought together. Importantly, I need to stress there were few Latino librarians at that time.

Drabinski: It's been noted that Elva Yañez[17] suggested revisions that had a significant impact on the thesaurus. Could you talk about her contributions?

Chabrán: Well, I think that her contributions were significant. She was a systems person. She was a strong advocate for not using the structure of the Library of Congress Subject Headings. She was really smart and a good systems person who helped us think through how to construct a thesaurus. She helped us make substantive changes. While Elva was not formally part of our team, she gave us a good outside perspective on what we were doing.

Drabinski: When you say she was more of a systems thinker, you mean library systems?

Chabrán: Yes, library systems, but her perspective was broader than libraries. One of her focuses in library schools was automation work. She had worked with the Spanish-speaking *Mental Health Database*.[18] This was originally a bibliography, but she helped develop the database. She helped them figure out how to do that conversion.

---

17. Elva Yañez is an environmental and health justice advocate. In the early 1970s she was a student worker at the Chicano Studies Library while studying for her library science masters at Mills College. She worked closely with Jose Antoino Arce to develop the Chicano Classification System and advised Richard Chabrán during the creation of the *Chicano Thesaurus*.

18. More information on the project can be found in Yanez, Elva Kocalis, and Edward John Kazlauskas. "The Spanish-Speaking Mental Health Research Center Bibliographic Data Base." *RQ* 19, no. 4 (1980): 354–59. http://www.jstor.org/stable/25826419.

Her work had an impact on what we were doing. She was somebody that was open and saw the need to not just do things traditionally. She helped us with that bridge of how to do the more cultural terms with machine language assistance.

Belantara: How do you feel the group's composition, in terms of race, class, geographic location, impacted the thesaurus?

Chabrán: I think it impacted it. So, the geographic location we did pretty good in terms of Chicano stuff. But as a criticism, I would say that we represented mostly the Southwest. So geographically, it was the Southwest. Those are the ones that we had access to.

Ethnically, it was aimed principally at Chicano material. Later on, we started to include more Latino groups. When I began working with the Center for Puerto Rican Studies at Hunter College at the City University of New York as part of the Inter University Consortium for Latino Studies, we began to include more Puerto Rican material. We never had as many ties with the Cuban American librarians.

In terms of gender, I think we had a fair amount of representation of both men and women. Although, I do think that in the beginning the leadership was more male-oriented. But when Lily took over, that changed.

Belantara: How did you decide on your methodological approach and what were some of the steps involved to get started?

Chabrán: Well, I think that the initial list was principally from three collections: UCLA, Santa Barbara, and Berkeley. At this point in time, the people that were in charge of those collections were very interested in collaborating. Previous to that time, some of those collections did not want to collaborate. They wanted to be like, "We're the best. We're gonna do it ourselves."

It was Francisco, Robert Trujillo—who wound up at Stanford, but at that time was at Santa Barbara—and myself. We said, "We're going to do this collaboratively."

We were just excited about being able to bring together this information. Once we did this and we produced a version of the thesaurus, then people could use the index. People were really excited about being able to use it, and they made some suggestions. It was like there was nothing there before and now we had something. People were excited!

That was basically it. And then we had the directions, the operational process that we weren't going to make it like a Library of Congress clone. It was going to be based on the simple things about how the thesaurus was structured. We took those three lists, and we did it. Today, maybe we would take three years and figure out some of the steps. We just did it and shared it with people.

Belantara: Did the Chicano Classification System, which was created by José Antonio Arce, have any impact on the generation of the thesaurus?

Chabrán: Oh yes, absolutely. It did. That was another one of those documents that we used while we were doing our work on the thesaurus. We had very little faith in the Library of Congress Subject Headings. And, specifically, these three libraries had developed some of their own subject headings. The thesaurus was a way of bringing that together.

Belantara: So, for each of those lists that came from the other Chicano Studies libraries, it was the librarians in charge there who were then just on their own generating lists of headings? Were they drawing those headings from the literature or from terms that they would just select on their own? How were they creating those?

Chabrán: Mostly from the literature. I'm not saying they never looked at the Library of Congress Subject Headings, but they weren't trying to reproduce that. In Anthropology, we have the terms, the emic and the etic. The emic is kind of like the people's term. The etic was the institutional term. So, we tried whenever we could to insert the emic. So, that was our philosophy.

Members of our group had been developing their own subject headings that they used principally for indexing or for providing access to the ephemeral material that they had. And we had these vertical files we needed to organize in some fashion. The headings that were used in those vertical files were some of the beginnings of the term lists. In some places they may have been on cards, but they had to still be made available to us.

At Berkeley we used our shelf heading list to develop our list. We had a shelf and we used those which were based on the Chicano Classification System. We used those as the basis for creating our list. And then, at Santa Barbara, they actually had a card catalog that had subject headings. So, Robert Trujillo had that put together. I don't think those lists exist anymore because sometimes they may have been on cards. We took those lists principally from UCLA, Berkeley, and Santa Barbara. They had developed these term lists and we took them and we merged them. I think that the actual bringing together was done by Robert Trujillo and Francisco and myself.

In the end, I ended up doing a good amount of that work. With their input, I merged the terms from all three libraries into one list. I would share copies of what I was doing with Robert and Francisco. We had this corpus of headings that were not what we ended up with at the end, but they were the items that we had for consideration to put into a thesaurus. When a group of us met with Ed Kazlauskas, a professor at the University of Southern California, he was working on software that could be used to develop a thesaurus. He told us, "Oh, there's this person who works in Mountain View whose name is Tom Holt. He has his own company."

So, then we met with him and this is, I think, a really important part of the project. In our discussions with him, Tom made it clear: "You do not want to do like a regular subject heading list."

It wasn't anything about the content of it, but he was saying, "At this time in history, there're a lot of problems with doing pre-coordinated terms. So, when you're developing this, you need to think about this as a database. When you work on your terms, think about them as standalone terms that can be combined to let searchers know where to get to."

So, we had a lot of conversations with him, saying what we wanted to do, and he said, "Okay, this is the way I propose doing it."

His system was kind of a basic system. The building blocks were there, but he had to do a lot of programming to get it to do what we wanted it to do. Because at that time, I was already going to library school or I had just finished, and I already had exposure to a lot of that—where we had to put together our own programs and use various programming languages. The indexers would send us the worksheets and we would forward them to Vort. We said, "Well, we don't really have the staff internally to be able to input all these worksheets."

So, we talked to Tom Holt and he said, "No problem. I have a person that can key all the worksheets and we'll charge you X amount." And we used some of the money from the library's publications account.

Drabinski: Can you tell us a little about how the subject terms were decided and what that process was like? Were there any disagreements about the best term?

Chabrán: I don't know that there was so much disagreement, but there were different ways of saying something. There were preferences for what you would use, different terms that'd say, "Well, there's that, but I'm not going to use that. This makes more sense to me."

And sometimes some of those had to do with, not all of them, but just an example, some of them had to do with using terms in Spanish that more reflected what people would look up. We just put things that made more sense to us. So, we included those kinds of terms. It was like, "Okay, you're putting this into some hierarchical term. Does that really make sense? Is that really part of that larger term? Should it be under that, or should it be under something else?"

I think that's kind of where we worked together on trying to figure that out. This has been done a long time ago. As I look back, that was in a really compressed time period, and probably one that we had not scheduled enough time for, but one that we were under the gun to do. So, if I look at it now, I could probably be pretty critical about some of our decisions. And I know that Lily can speak to this better, but I know there was a point at which she had somebody work on the LGBT terms.

And I would think the thesaurus is like a living thing. And I don't think necessarily when we did it, that it was the end of the dialogue. It was just the beginning. So, I see it as something living and I hope that it changes. One of the other things that it did was that it ended up not getting used just for our index. It got used for collections in different universities. It got accepted as a kind of a subject heading. And by the Library of Congress, if you can use alternative headings in the MARC record, you can use *Chicano Thesaurus* terms.

Drabinski: Can you tell us a little about any of the terms in the thesaurus that were most meaningful to you or to the researchers?

Chabrán: So, remember, this is like 1976 or 1975, there was a debate about *Illegal aliens*. We were using *Undocumented workers* for a long time before that and people embraced that. So, it's like, okay, did we use *Undocumented persons* or *Workers*? So, there were discussions about that. But that was a term that I think really captured it.

Then, there were the terms that were the types of literary things that were going on. There's the term that's used, I don't know if you're familiar with that, but it's *Chicanesca*, which is, like, literature that's about the Chicano experience, but it's written by people who are not.

Another term that I think was really important was the term *Chicana*. That was important because that was, like, not just signifying a gender, it was like an identity. We had a group of undergraduate women that did a bibliography called *Bibliography of Writings on La Mujer.*[19] They identified themselves as Chicanas. Some of them became librarians. That was another thing which was really important.

---

19. University of California, B. Chicano Studies Library., Rodríguez, M., Rios, G., Portillo, C. (1976). *Bibliography of Writings on La Mujer*. Berkeley, CA: Chicano Studies Library, University of California at Berkeley. https://catalog.hathitrust.org/Record/101170818/Home.

Another term we embraced was *Land grants*. We found out that, legally, *Land grants* can only apply in certain situations that are sanctioned by the government. That was a real lesson there, but we still use the term.

Drabinski: Once you finalized your word list, what was the next step?

Chabrán: Well, we published it. We put it together and published it in house. We made copies of it and sent it out to all the indexers. Eventually, it got revised a couple of times and, much later, it got accepted as one of the alternative subject lists approved by the Library of Congress that you could use in a MARC field that shows local headings.

Drabinski: When did you know that you were done with the thesaurus?

Chabrán: Oh, we're not. I think that because of the number of terms that we used, the indexing was richer. Not just the terminology, but the application was more generous in terms of what it was about.

Belantara: How did that make you feel once you had completed or made your first version of the thesaurus? How did that make you feel, A) to get to that stage and then B) to see other people, other libraries using it and people being able to discover things that had perhaps been hidden before due to lack of appropriate description?

Chabrán: I think we all felt very gratified, but I think at that point we were so busy with so many things that we never really stopped. We were really happy, but it was always more like, okay, that's done. Here's the next thing. So, it was not like, "Okay, well we did that, now we can rest."

There was always a struggle to keep it going, to do the next thing. And we got the first Index published by G.K. Hall and then the Chicano Studies Library had to immediately keep publishing it. It was always something. It was non-ending. We wanted to do this database like a national one. There were always things to do. So, we never stopped.

Belantara: What were some of the reactions that people shared? Once you printed the thesaurus, how did you go about getting it out to other institutions or other libraries?

Chabrán: The first widely distributed version was published as part of the index. But we had a separate one that we made available, and a lot of people purchased that. It was probably, I don't know, wasn't that much. I want to say it was like seven or ten dollars, I don't know. But it wasn't that much. I just remember us getting together. And my reaction and theirs was just to say thank you. Thank you. We did it! I mean, there was no money involved. The thing that struck me the most was that it was being used. And now to this day, people said, "Until then we couldn't do this and then all of a sudden, we could do all this research."

To me, that was the most meaningful thing.

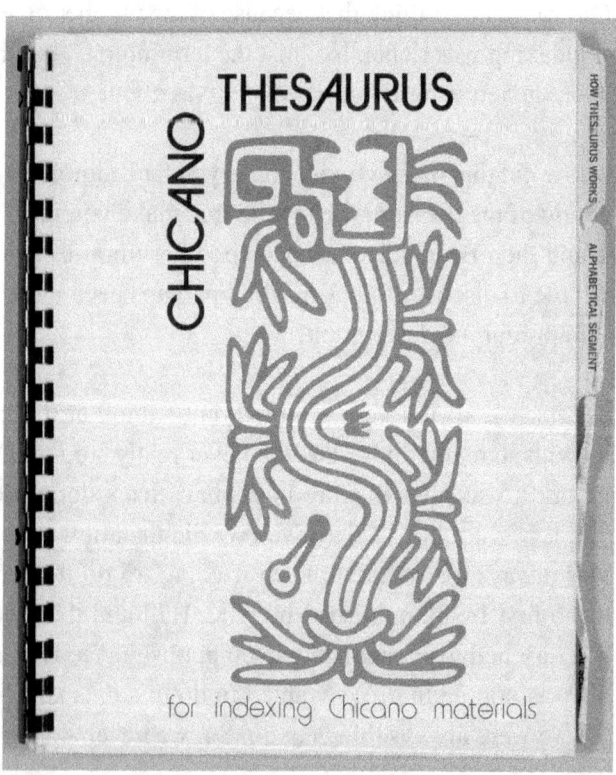

Figure 2. Cover page of the Chicano Thesaurus published in 1981.

Belantara: Did you apply for or receive funding for the *Chicano Thesaurus*? What were the costs associated with the project?

Chabrán: When we first said we're going to do this project, the *Chicano Periodical Index*, which the thesaurus was part of, we knew about this place called the Rosenberg Foundation in San Francisco. We went to the campus office and we said, "We want to apply to get some money."

They said, "Well, you can't. Our relationship with them is such that they won't receive proposals directly from you. You have to do it through the library."

And so, I said okay. So, I went to see the University Librarian and we told him what we wanted to do. I believe it was just me and him. And then he said, "Well, we will not support you in that effort unless you use the Library of Congress Subject Headings."

So, I said, "Well, we are going to use our own terms."

And so, he said, "Well, I'm sorry, I can't support you."

And that was the end of that conversation. Then we remembered that we had this revenue that we got from the microfilming of newspapers in our publications account. That turned out to be a good amount of money. So, we used that money. The majority of those funds were used to pay for the consulting of Vort Corporation and for the computing time, and for the data entry. So, we really didn't ever get outside money to do that. It was just paid for that way.

Belantara: And how did the group gather institutional support? Was there ever any kind of pushback?

Chabrán: These people that worked on indexing, the majority of them, I would say almost all of them (I can't say a hundred percent) were librarians. So, they used their professional time because as librarians, you have to do professional service or whatever. They used that to contribute their time to doing this work. I don't remember any of them actually asking their supervisor to do that. That may have been true, for example, at the University of Texas at the Benson Latin American Collection where they already kind were committed to this kind of activity. But I think most of the people didn't ask and they just did it. And probably a lot of them would say they did it on their own time. There was really no pushback.

Afterwards, of course, a lot of them thought it was great because we tried to give every institution as much credit as we could. So, they got something out of it. Administrators didn't put money into it, but they got a lot of recognition afterwards that they had contributed. It was right there on the first pages of the index that there were all these institutions.

Drabinski: The thesaurus is now in use in commercial products. It's been implemented by the Library of Congress as part of its MARC record standards. Can you say something about how you feel about this mainstream adoption of your work since it sounds like from the beginning it was sort of a project that was counter to those systems?

Chabrán: How do I say this? I don't think we ever wanted to be oppositional. I mean, we didn't see ourselves as being against any of that. It was just, like, it didn't work for us. I now worry not that index itself, but just that as time goes on, I see less people, librarians, being able to devote the kind of time that it takes to really become specialists in this. I was lucky, man.

I was able to devote my whole career to a particular area that we call Chicano Studies or Latino Studies. And now, my colleagues that I talked to, they have like ten different subject areas they're doing. They don't really know deeply about what most of them are. They have good tools to be able to cover them, but I got to know most of the people that were writing the literature. I got to know the literature really closely.

So, I kind of worry about that more. At the same time, there are fantastic things that are being done. The literature is in a wholly different place. That gives me great gratitude.

Belantara: What were your hopes going forward at the time that you passed it on to Lillian?

Chabrán: I'm trying to remember, but I think that Francisco actually was working closely with her. I mean, there was overlap between them.

She'll be able to tell you more than me. We've always had, and continue to have, a really close working relationship.

Especially, for a long time she would call me a few times a week and we would go over questions. Maybe we can consider this a kind of mentorship. There were always a lot of questions, but like I said, I think she took it and ran with it, right.

She has special talents as an editor. She's a really great editor. She's really been able to upgrade the database from what it was. I would say she's curated the database and the project.

So, she's taken it from being what was on this minicomputer and then she took it from there and worked with programmers to get it on a personal computer using different kinds of database tools. Maybe she doesn't even think of it that way, but I know through the years, she's really taken and curated in such a way that keeps it together, the integrity.

Belantara: If you could talk to your younger self at the start of your career and your start of working on the *Chicano Thesaurus*, what would you tell your younger self?

Chabrán: I don't know what the right term is, but we were outspoken, sometimes a little bit brash or whatever. And so, I think that I would be softer, not so much with my colleagues, but trying to get other people to work together. I think that's one thing I would think of.

I'll also think about how this work was kind of directed at Chicanos, but a better way of bringing in, which we eventually did a lot, for example, Puerto Ricans and Cubans and Central Americans. I would say how do we do that, finding other ways in which we could have brought people together. And we did it when we could. But I think what hurt us was to not be able to get outside funding. If we were able to get those initial grants, we would've done a lot more of that. So, we did it, kind of, on a shoestring.

If I talked to my younger self I would say, how do we, how can we get more funds to bring people together more? We could have done a lot more. I have to say that even though a large part of the project was using automation, people at that point didn't have the tools that we have now to communicate, the personal computers and forget about social media and all that. That didn't exist. Using the tools that we had, I think we did pretty good. But if we had more time together, we could have done more, and we could have done it better.

So, that's the main thing I would think. I remain in awe of my colleagues that were able to put in so much time and investment into something they were not going to get paid for.

Belantara: It's incredibly inspiring and impressive because despite not having the funding and all of the support that we wish that you would've had, hey, the thesaurus exists and continues to make different research more widely accessible.

Chabrán: But I want to say, I think I had told you I had the opportunity for about twenty years to teach part-time at the University of Arizona and their School of Information. In the latter part of the classes that I taught there, we always focused on the ways of telling and ways of knowing.

I tried really hard to impress upon my students that if you want to make change, it's not just some bureaucratic thing. You have to be willing to hear, to listen, and to know that your own way of knowing is not the way everybody knows. And if you're not willing to do that, no matter what kind of library work you do, it will not be successful. And so, to me, a profound thing about, if you listen, you have to realize that people have different ways of knowing, they have different ways of telling.

And so, to me, the ways of telling, to capture that, you have to have a system that's willing to capture those different ways of telling and knowing. And I continue to believe, I'm sorry, but the Library of Congress fails on both counts.

They do a lot. I don't want to discount them or anything, but if you don't do that, then you're always going to be the conqueror. We're bringing this in, and this is the way it's going to be, and bam. It's going to put it on the floor, and that's it. But that's not a very progressive way to capture things. And to me, I already understood this, but it really was underscored for me when I taught the Native American students, and they talk about this a lot. It's not that they want to be excluded, but what they believe and their way of seeing the world is different.

They don't want their ways of cosmology to be just viewed as folklore. Not something that's not real, but it's real. You have to, it has to really emanate from that. And if you believe that, then every part of librarianship is affected by it.

I think that the thesaurus is one little piece of that. People like to think about diversity as something that's not very deep, but if it's serious, it's got to go all the way through all of these systems. So that's that.

Lillian Castillo-Speed on the Chicano Thesaurus

Biography

Lillian Castillo-Speed grew up in La Puente, in the San Gabriel Valley of Southern California. She received her B.A. in English from the University of California at Riverside and her Master's degree from the School of Library and Information Studies at the University of California, Berkeley in 1983. She worked on a contract job for a year to catalog rare Spanish language imprints from a convent in Mexico before accepting the position of Library Coordinator of the Chicano Studies Library at UC Berkeley in 1984. In 1991, Lillian was named the Head Librarian of the three libraries in the Ethnic Studies Department: Asian American Studies

Library, Native American Studies Library, and Chicano Studies Library. In 1997, the three libraries became one Ethnic Studies Library.

Since 1984, Lillian has been the Database Manager of the Chicano Database, a project begun at the Chicano Studies Library that is a bibliographic resource distributed to libraries across the country. She has also been the Managing Editor of the Publications Unit of the Chicano Studies Library and of the Ethnic Studies Library. She is the editor of *Latina: Women's Voices from the Borderlands* (Simon and Schuster, 1995), among other editorial roles. In 1996, Lillian Castillo-Speed received the REFORMA Librarian of the Year Award and in 2012, she received the Distinguished Librarian Award from the Librarians Association of the University of CaliforniaBerkeley Division.

About the Interview

The following transcribed interview of Lillian Castillo-Speed took place on June 10, 2022, as part of the *Ways of Knowing Oral History Project*. The interview was initially transcribed by using transcription software before being corrected by Belantara and Drabinski. Care was taken to not alter the original transcription's contents. However, the editors have formatted the following to improve readability and provided footnotes for clarity where appropriate. The original transcription and oral history recording can be accessed through New York University Libraries.[1]

Transcript from the *Ways of Knowing Oral History Project*

Interviewee: Lillian Castillo-Speed, Head Librarian of the Ethnic Studies Library at the University of California, Berkeley.
Interviewers: Emily Drabinski & Amanda Belantara
Date: June 10, 2022
Location: Virtual Interview; University of California, Berkeley

---

1. Lillian Castillo-Speed's oral history and original transcript can be accessed through New York University Libraries. https://search.library.nyu.edu/permalink/01NYU_INST/1d6v258/alma990098389910107871.

Amanda Belantara: Today we're interviewing Lillian Castillo-Speed, Head Librarian of the Ethnic Studies Library at the University of California, Berkeley. The interview was conducted for the *Ways of Knowing Oral History Project*. It was recorded virtually on June 10th, 2022. The interviewers are Amanda Belantara and Emily Drabinski.

Belantara: Hi Lillian, we're so glad to have this opportunity to talk with you today. We'd like to start by hearing a little from you about your background and education, and what led you to become a librarian.

Lillian Castillo-Speed: That could be a long story! I was born in East Los Angeles. I grew up in the San Gabriel Valley and was the first in our family to go to college. I went to UC Riverside. I was an English major, and later decided to go to library school. That's the long part of the story. I ended up at UC Berkeley, and I got my master's in library science degree there in 1983.

Belantara: How did you decide to go into librarianship?

Castillo-Speed: My husband and I moved to UC Santa Barbara because he was getting his PhD there, and our son Nathan had just been born. I had wonderful years with my son as he was growing up. When he went to preschool, I needed to do something else. I had not finished my graduate work in English at that point. I found an ad in the paper to be a volunteer at a high school library, and I went every Thursday. I looked forward to it and got dressed up for that one Thursday. An actual job opening came up in another high school and I got recommendations to apply there. I got that job as a library tech. There was a librarian there, and she had her own office.

Susan and I, the other library tech, didn't have our own offices, but we were always out at the front desk where all the action was with the students. I wanted to go and get some more skills as a library tech because I had no skills. I hadn't been trained in library stuff. This was way back before the internet. I found out that there was a library tech training program at Santa Barbara City College. I took the bus, walked in the building, and they said, "No, we don't have that program anymore."

And I said, "Well, do you know of any other place that has a library tech program?"

Because there was no way to just look it up on Google. But they said, "Oh, well, go talk to the librarian on the campus."

So I went into the library, there was a woman at the front desk, and I told her, "I want to get library tech training."

And she said, "Well, do you have a bachelor's degree?"

And I said, "Yes."

She says, "Well, you should go to library school."

And that was the first time that that possibility ever came into my head that I could just go to library school. So, I applied to different places. When I got an offer from Berkeley and a little scholarship for that program, then we decided after my husband's PhD program was over, we got a moving van, and we moved up to Berkeley so I could get my library degree there.

Belantara: What year was it when you started your library degree?

Castillo-Speed: 1981. Yeah, it was hot, August time when we moved into married student housing on the campus, and very, very old buildings. It was wonderful to be in Berkeley.

Belantara: When you started the program, was there anything that you found most interesting about the field?

Castillo-Speed: Well, I was looking forward to anything having to do with digital. What did we call it? Computer, we used to call it computer stuff back then because that was just coming up, and that's when I thought I would just get a basic degree for librarianship. But then I ended up taking, what do they call them, independent units in learning how to do some software program. I can't remember what it was, but I got a unit for learning how to use that program. I thought that's where things were going and that's where I should be. I should be learning how to do computer stuff.

Emily Drabinski: Can you tell us how you came to work at the Chicano Studies Library?

Castillo-Speed: At library school I had a friend named Peter Latino, and he recommended a course that was in the library school curriculum called Ethnic Bibliography. It was taught by a librarian on campus named Francisco García Ayvens. And I thought, "Well, I'll do it."

I didn't really know anything about it, but I signed up for the class and that's how I found out about the Chicano Studies Library, because I was going to go to that class. Part of the class was giving tours of different ethnic libraries in the area, public and academic, just anything that was some ethnic focused libraries. His library, the Chicano Studies Library, was one of them. When I walked in, that was the first time I'd been on campus that changed my life, walking through that door, which I can see in my mind very clearly: 104 Wheeler Hall. And I became a volunteer. I was in the class and just wanted to do everything that Francisco was doing. He showed me collection development and everything that he was working on; he is a lifelong friend. That was very important for me in my life, in my career.

Drabinski: Can you tell us anything about what sort of feeling on campus was around Chicano issues at that time? Is this still 1981?

Castillo-Speed: Yes. I was not that connected with, as a graduate student, to that much activity, like marches or anything like that. So, I was not really drawn into anything. But when I decided to focus on Chicano librarianship, I took a class in Chicano history and just became more aware of the history and the issues, the concerns, and where I was in that arc of history. And also through Francisco, because he recommended books for me to read to just make me more aware of my history. I had been taking Spanish ever since high school because I'm not a native speaker.

We didn't get Spanish when we were young, but my grandmother always wanted us to speak Spanish. And so that was a personal goal of mine, to please her and to try to become a Spanish speaker. When I was in college, too, I took Spanish. So then also when I was in library school, I took a summer class in Spanish. So, I just kind of kept that going. And also there were tutors and teachers that had classes offsite and you'd pay for them, and then we'd speak in Spanish—that kind of thing. Once I knew that I wanted to be in the Chicano Studies librarianship world, then I tried to learn more about Chicano studies and Chicano history.

> *"...if we don't do it, nobody's going to do it. So, we've got to do it."*

Drabinski: Can you tell us about your initial thoughts about the need for a specialized vocabulary for these collections?

Castillo-Speed: That came as I was in library school, and again, I was being mentored by Francisco and also by Richard Chabrán, who at that time was the Chicano Studies Librarian at UCLA. They were both part of the Chicano periodical indexing project. And so, I started to learn about that just from being in Francisco's office. I just remember him telling me everything, telling me what he was working on, what it was. I didn't realize till later that that was the very beginning.

I mean that he was in the middle of a lot of transitions there, from there being a network of Chicano librarians who wanted to create an indexing project so that Chicano movement journals would be accessible, to reference tools. Because at that point, they were not included in the *Reader's Guide*.[2] So, one of the transitions, there was a librarian group that worked on this, but then I realized that the project became more and more centered at Berkeley and that Francisco was the head of that. He

---

2. An index of popular periodicals that was heavily used by libraries. *Readers' Guide to Periodical Literature.* Minneapolis: H. W. Wilson Co.

was the one that was keeping it going for the most part with Richard's help, getting help from the other people, but it wasn't like a cooperative kind of thing. They were there making sure that it kept going.

So, that was a transition. The index was being published by G.K. Hall, but then they stopped publishing it. And so, the Chicano Studies Library itself, which had its own publications unit, decided to publish it on their own. So that was another transition. It's only looking back that I see that when Francisco was telling me about these things, the project was in transition on different fronts.

And, back to your question, the vocabulary, at the beginning—it just seemed like if you're going to have an indexing project and you're going to index, then you're going to have to decide how you are going to apply subject headings to the things that you're indexing. So, the *Chicano Thesaurus* was a tool, a necessary tool. It wasn't like, oh, people got together thinking "Wouldn't it be nice to have a nice vocabulary?"

It was something that they actually needed. It was something necessary. In order to have an indexing project, you had to figure out what a project was going to use in order to give subject access to materials. So, I didn't see the thesaurus itself as being something that you just create on your own, just because it would be nice to have a Chicano controlled vocabulary. It's because they actually just needed it. But it did interest me, and I think now maybe because I had been an English major, I was interested in just language in itself. So, I think that's why I wrote an article when I was in library school. I wrote a paper; it was actually a paper for a class to get credit. It was based on my interviews with Francisco and Richard and other librarians, and it was called "The Usefulness of the *Chicano Thesaurus*."[3]

And so, I just wrote about it and what I was learning at that point. So that experience of having to write a paper—I had to write a paper— so I had to go interview other people, I had to take notes, I had to get a bibliography; all that focused my attention on the thesaurus at that time.

---

3. Castillo-Speed, L. (1984). "The Usefulness of the *Chicano Thesaurus* for Indexing Chicano Materials." In *Biblio-Politica: Chicano Perspectives on Library Service in the United States*, 169-178. Chicano Studies Publications Unit.

That's how I remember my first experience with the thesaurus and why it was important.

Drabinski: Did it feel, when you were learning about it, like a political project or just a utilitarian one?

Castillo-Speed: During that time when I took that class, met Francisco, walked in the door, from that point on, for me, it was all political. I mean the work, the space, the library itself, when I heard about the history of it and how it came to be out of a political movement. So, it's hard to separate that work from what was not political because it was political. It was all political.

Drabinski: Can you tell us a little more about the *Chicano Periodical Index*?

Castillo-Speed: Yes, that was the beginning of the Chicano Database. There have been some articles written about that time period. I'm just trying to think of forty, fifty years ago, of what the state of computer technology was and what it is now. So, back then there were key punch operators, punch cards; I'm trying to think of the terminology. In order to write a program, and we did learn this in library school, we did have a class where we had to learn how to write a program. We didn't go to a keyboard and type in anything. You had to go to a machine, and it was a keyboard, a key punch.

Once these cards were punched out with the little holes that indicated the program you were trying to write or the program lines for a program, you had to submit it. On the Berkeley campus there was a place to take them and put them in a box. And a technician there, or student, whatever, would then go and put it into the mainframe of the campus and it would get entered. And then two or three days later, you'd go and you'd try to pick up and see if the coding was accepted or if there were mistakes in it or something. So that was how it was when I was in library school.

The *Chicano Periodical Index* project began around the time when things had to be done that way. So that, from what I understand, indexers have something in hand, a journal, looking at an article, and then they'd fill out worksheets, and the worksheets were sent to a central place. And then from there, they were coded into a mainframe. I wasn't there at that time so I'm just imagining how that would work. But again, this was at this transition time when I found out all about this. Things were changing.

Okay, about the periodical indexing project. There was a group of librarians, in California mostly, some from Texas, I think also in Arizona and New Mexico, that agreed to become indexers. They filled out worksheets and were assigned different titles of Chicano journals. They were librarians who had access to subscriptions to these journals. They signed up, and they sent in the worksheets. It ended up being that Berkeley was the processing place and Francisco would be the one to make sure people were doing their assignments, and then putting them into a computer program.

Then there was a company called Vort Corporation, owned by Tom Holt, and he was the person who was contracted to make this data come out into, what is it called, "printer ready" pages that were then sent out to G.K. Hall, the publisher. And the pages that were printed out of the index were the actual ones that came right out of the computer printer, formatted. They became the pages of the book of the index. The first two volumes of the index were the result of that process.

Belantara: It sounds like Francisco was heavily involved in terms of coordinating and organizing the group. Did all of this work occur in different places? Did people ever come together to do some of the indexing work? And when people were working on this, do you have any idea what the atmosphere was like and how people managed to actually get the work done?

Castillo-Speed: First of all, I have to say that I was not there at the beginnings of that, so I don't know. Richard Chabrán would know more about the meetings. It wasn't that easy to get together, I assume, during that time period. But the people that are listed as indexers in the early volumes, I've known most of them through the years, and I know that they are committed. I can see why they would be part of this project.

I'm assuming that they thought it was very important, and they did have to make it part of their work time or their professional development time. I know people would list themselves, like when they were coming up for reviews or something, they would say, "Oh, I'm an indexer for the *Chicano Periodical Index*."

So that was something that could motivate them a little bit. But I think it was mostly because they thought it was an important thing to do. If it were me, I'm just projecting on to what I'm thinking they might be thinking, is that if I knew that a sizable and important portion of intellectual printed, published history was not accessible, and it was because they were not mainstream and that they had to do something not mainstream in order for that material to be visible, then I would also feel motivated by that thinking. Like, if we don't do it, nobody's going to do it. So, we've got to do it.

Seeing how things turned out afterwards, my take on it would be that that impulse or that motivation was strong there at the beginning. But, as time went on, I think it became more focused with Richard Chabrán and Francisco García and that people saw them as the leaders, and they actually were the ones—if it wasn't for those two people taking that leadership role and even putting more of their time and making more connections and try to get funding and those kinds of things, I don't think the project would still be going on. I think it was the leadership that kept things going.

Belantara: In your article, and in some of Richard's writings as well, there's mention of the Chicano Classification System. Did that come before the thesaurus? And if so, was that used in the creation of the thesaurus?

Castillo-Speed: I'm not sure which one came first. I do know that Richard Chabrán used to be the librarian at Chicano Studies Library at UC

Berkeley before Francisco. I'm assuming it was during that time because the classification system preceded Francisco. It could have been, like, almost at the same time. It was in that same time period. Maybe it's kind of an analogy: the periodical indexing project needed a tool, needed the thesaurus. The Chicano Studies Library, when the students were starting to organize it and found a space and a reading room and had bookshelves and they started to collect books, they needed to start figuring out what order we were going to put these things in. How do we organize this?

And they were not library school students. Richard himself, he was an anthropology major and got pulled into this. The way I heard it, they sent him to library school. The group needed somebody to go to and they figured out who's the most likely one that can go and get library training and come back to help make this library work. So, Richard went to library school. But during that time period, the students, and I'm not sure if Richard was part of that at that point, but anyway, they consulted with librarians in the main library for help. How do you do this? How do you find those numbers that you put on the back of books?

I've heard that they were helpful, and they told them about the Library of Congress Classification system, okay? But the students saw right away that if they used the Library of Congress Classification System, everything in the Chicano Studies Library would be under E184.5 something. And they wouldn't have that.

That would just be so unusable that they just couldn't do that. So anyway, they decided to take over the classification system on their own. So, for instance, music has the ML classification. So, they made music, Chicano music. So, the Chicano music books would be under M, the Chicano art books would be under N, the literature would be under variations of the P class rather than putting everything in under E184. They had to create that. They made a modification of it. I do have a copy of, I think it's the original copy that was printed out on computer paper with lines on it and holes on the side. It's been marked up and edited.

When the Ethnic Studies Library was formed, the Chicano Studies Library became part of the Ethnic Studies Library. And I actually gave [the Chicano Classification System] to our cataloger. The cataloger had to use it to understand how the Chicano studies collection was organized because that's how it had been organized from the beginning. I'm not sure which one came first, but it was all during that time period.

I wasn't there at the time, but that's the legend, the lore, the history that pulls me in. I repeat this story to people who come when I give classes, library classes for students coming in, and I tell them the history of the library and the history of the collections and everything. I've repeated the story many times. While we're talking about it, the students came upon the class of E and PS, which is literature, language and literature. And they were trying to find a place to put Chicano literature. And at the time, and I guess it still is, that if they put it in the PS class, they would have to make a distinction between things written in English and things written in Spanish or any other language. And they wouldn't have that at all.

For them Chicano literature, this is very political too, could be any language; that was just an artificial division. So, they created PX as Chicano literature; and we still have PX. I mean, that is where we have our Chicano literature: on the shelves in the Chicano Studies Collection, at the Ethnic Studies Library. If I have time, I always try to tell that story because they took it on their own. I mean, they saw what the structure was supposed to be, but they made it their own. They altered it; they changed it so it could reflect what they wanted to show, how they wanted things to look, and how the world should look from their point of view. Because the shelves of a library are like a world in themselves with all these different areas.

Belantara: In your article, "The Usefulness of the *Chicano Thesaurus* for Indexing Chicano Materials," you wrote: "It was to be what Chicano librarians had long dreamed of, a subject heading list of their own, which would provide vocabulary control." Could you talk more about this dream?

Castillo-Speed: I was making an assumption about what I think would've been their dream. But when I say dream, I think I was thinking more in terms of when the *Chicano Periodical Index* project was conceived, the way it started there—it sounds like for decades—but more just when people started to focus on it and think that an indexing project would be a great thing to do. I think that's as long as they dreamed about it. And also, I think it goes back to what I said about the PX classification, that it would be something of their own that wouldn't be mandated by what was established already or what was supposed to be. And that often would leave out things that were important to Chicano culture or Chicano experience, Chicano history. Just because they didn't fit. That's what I was thinking.

They did dream of it, and they did see it as important because then it would be their way of expressing themselves.

"The way people are named, or language that's used to describe people is very powerful. It could be very hurtful, or it could be empowering... It's very emotional that people can be classified, cataloged by the words that are used to describe them, and they lose their humanity."

Belantara: Related to that, what does vocabulary mean for access?

Castillo-Speed: That's a big question. I mean, a lot of things come to mind. One is very political, right? And very current. The way people are named, or language that's used to describe people is very powerful. It could be very hurtful, or it could be empowering. Language, I think, is potent.

When you're dealing with it, you have to be careful. Let's say a group of people decide to create a language, create a list of subject headings, then every word becomes important—because that means that you're choosing that one as acceptable to a group of people. And you're just one; maybe you're like a handful of people, but how do you know it's going to be acceptable to a lot of people, to everybody who might read that? It's very emotional that people can be classified, cataloged by the words that are used to describe them, and they lose their humanity.

At the same time, if you have the courage, and I'm not saying me, I'm saying the people who've created the idea of even having a thesaurus, and say, like, we're going to include all these words that maybe, oh, my grandmother used or these words that I grew up with and these words that we know among us that we use all the time. Even if they sound, whatever, foreign or clunky or odd to other people, we're going to just say yes, even the word Chicano.

Even just thinking of that, to call yourself Chicano or call anything Chicano, you're already taking a stand against a lot of other stuff. With each word, I mean I'm sure some of them were very easy to figure out, like, okay, they didn't have to think about that much, but I think some of the words they had to think about, oh, okay, we're going to include that word. Okay, yes. Okay, what's the related term to that? Oh yeah, there's another term. So yeah, that's language, and it is very important.

I mean that's a no brainer, but I'm having in mind the more recent battles about the term *Illegal aliens* and how there's certain language that was, and is, used by the establishment and how there's other language that could be used instead. And how that first term is so hurtful, even if you're not in that category of people that the term is trying to describe, it is hurtful, and it just shows how powerful a language is. So, I guess the people that were putting together the thesaurus were pretty aware that they were creating something that some people would not accept, but because of the material that they were trying to index, it made sense. The material brought up these words. If there was a concept that they were trying to convey, it'd be better to use a term that was not hurtful than to use one that was hurtful. Why pick that other one if you could pick something else?

Belantara: Can you mention a few of the terms that might be most meaningful to you personally or to researchers that you work with?

Castillo-Speed: The one off the top of my head I can think of is the one that's used or the other terms that are used instead of *Illegal aliens*. From the beginning there was the term *Undocumented workers*. Later, as the material evolved or there were other types of materials, it wasn't just the worker aspect that was important or needed to be described, but it was also the people that were living in the United States who were undocumented. So, then we've added the term *Undocumented residents*. And then I think we've had, for a long time, *Undocumented children*.

So, just to give you the other side of *Illegal aliens*—over the years, another term that's come up was *Racial profiling*. And just to mention that the way that we do the periodical index, now it's the database. There are index terms which are in the thesaurus, but there are also supplementary terms. And those are terms that are people, places, or things. That's where we would put a term that was coming up and we weren't sure was going to become an index term yet. So, at the time when a lot of news articles and conversations were about racial profiling, we made it a supplemental term. Sometimes what happens is that another term takes over. You decide, okay, this is going to be *Racial profiling*, and then it turns out it's going to be another term. It becomes like, oh no, everybody's calling it this, so then you have to change over. So that's why there's this waiting period. Finally, it took hold, it became a term. And so, we added that.

I'm trying to think of ones that I wasn't involved in adding. There was a project to actually add two areas to the thesaurus that needed to be fleshed out or we needed to have more terms for.

Belantara: How did you actually start getting involved or being the person in charge of the thesaurus?

Castillo-Speed: Well, that came with the periodical index. It was 1984. Francisco decided to resign in order to go back to LA to be with his family, and I was working as a cataloger on a temporary project in San Francisco. But I was always coming back to the Chicano Studies Library to continue doing volunteer work there and hanging out.

When he resigned, he gave me a little bit of a heads up on that. But anyway, I applied to be the temporary librarian to take over from his position, and I was named the temporary librarian. And then, when the permanent position opened up, I applied for that, and I got the job. With the job came everything that Francisco was doing, which was coordinating the periodical index, which at that point was becoming the database.

There was a transition that was beginning around that time. And with that was the thesaurus. I mean that they're intricately connected. You can't separate one from the other. So, I had to keep up with working on that, too. Just to be clear, I was never alone. I was not left on my own to do this. Francisco was always available by phone. Richard, who was still the Chicano Studies librarian at the UCLA Chicano Studies Research Center, was also always available by phone. I still remember the phone number!

I think I talked to him daily because he was in the same UC library system. He knew how things worked, and he was also mentoring me on being a librarian at UC, not just the Index. During those years, and still to some extent today, I don't see myself as the one person totally in charge of the project. Sadly, Francisco passed away in 2018, but I see Richard and I as equally being in charge of what's going on. I took over from Francisco, but never left on my own to figure out what to do.

Belantara: When you first started taking over some of the work that Francisco was doing with the thesaurus and the database, did you have some learning curves? How did you go about acquiring the necessary skills and knowledge?

Castillo-Speed: Oh, my gosh. I know there's probably a lot of things, but what first comes to mind is the equipment, the computer, the system. I think by the time I met Francisco he had already purchased a system called the Alpha Micro 1000. I don't know if Alpha Micro is still out there or if anybody's heard of it, but it was revolutionary at the time. It ran on AlphaBASIC, its own version of the BASIC language.

What was different about it was that you could have several terminals connected to the one mother computer. And so that meant that he could have one terminal in our, I couldn't even call it a computer room, but it was just the other side of his office. And then he had a monitor in his office, a monitor in the reading room, and different people could be adding data to it. And that whole thing about different terminals was like, whoa, that was really neat!

The other thing I want to mention is that he told me that he had used one year's allotment for collection development to buy the Alpha Micro. I think it was like $10,000 at the time. That means there were no books bought, no serials. The whole book budget went to that to just buy that one system. So, he took a chance. I mean, he bought it, and with that came the programmer person that I mentioned, Tom Holt. So, the learning curve that I have in mind right now was working with Tom Holt. He was the kind of person that... Looking back on it, he was not the most pleasant person, but he taught me a whole lot. At times he seemed impatient. But I think I needed to have somebody to be impatient and not mess things up. Because I think he was trying to let me know that I was in charge. Francisco wasn't there, Richard wasn't, I was the one that could be messing things up if I didn't do it right.

I remember this one night, it was the end of the day, but for some reason I started some program, and I think he had said something like, "Okay, just let it run until something else happens."

Okay, so then I waited and waited and waited and waited, and I was so afraid that if I touched anything, I was going to mess something up. I was there for a couple of hours after work. I don't know how long I was there, but I always remember that feeling that I was going to mess it up either by not doing something or by doing something. I don't know how I got home that day or how I slept that night. It turned out to be okay. But I think he wanted me to be in that kind of state so that I wasn't going to do something rash or mess things up. But anyway, that was a big learning curve for me. And then just trying to learn everything I could.

Again, this was when we didn't have desktop computers. We couldn't go look up how to do things. You had to rely on somebody like the programmer to tell you whether you're doing it okay or not. Another thing I learned was to be very precise with programmers and try to speak their language even though I'm not a programmer. I think instead of just saying, okay, I wanted to do this and this and this, I could be very precise, and that would help things. And then the programmer would respond to that positively, and I could work better with them. That was a learning experience for me.

Belantara: Can you paint a picture of what it was like when you actually sat down at this state-of-the-art system and how you would get started with work?

Castillo-Speed: Some of the work was inputting data from worksheets that were sent in, and then that started to dwindle a bit. But there were worksheets from outside indexers when I first started. And then a lot of it was us, myself, putting in indexing, putting material, putting data in. And then we also hired students after the worksheets were already edited. I would figure out that, okay, these are good to put in, and then the students would just put the data in.

So yeah, the way it looked was completely different. Small screen, all black. You're working in BASIC language, it was kind of like DOS[4], but it was even more basic than DOS. It was the Alpha Micro version of BASIC. You had to learn that. For what we were doing, it was repeating the same process over and over again. I didn't have to learn a whole lot of other stuff, but there was a template.

I can't even remember if there was something that was there and we filled it in or if you input something and then something would come out next line or hit return. I can't even remember. But I do know that at that point, it was all numbers. I mean, for the most part, it was numbers. Let me back up. What I meant was, if you're inputting a title, you would type in the title because that was probably a unique piece of information for the database.

If there are a lot of poems, there would probably be a lot of them called mother or love or something like that, right? So that title could be repeated, but often the title was not repeated. So that would be unique. You need to type it in. And then we used a number for an author and so you would type in the number for that author. I can't remember if it would show up on the screen—you type it in and then it'll tell you what the

---

4. DOS is a disk operating system created by Microsoft.

number was and you type it. That I can't remember. But I do know that the terms themselves all had numbers.

So, *Chicanas* was 638, like Richard's phone number; that was always going to stay in my brain. 638 is *Chicanas*. I probably could remember some other ones if I thought about it. And then you'd hit return, and then you could review it. And then, when you were ready to make a printout camera-ready, that was camera-ready pages, and you'd print it out. You'd hear the printer typing it out. Thank you for inviting me to remember that because it's so different now.

Belantara: Over the years you worked with a group of people to revise the thesaurus. How were revisions decided upon with each new edition of the thesaurus? As you were making these revisions, were the changes and decisions documented as well?

Castillo-Speed: That's a good question. I think I documented everything I did on the database in a series of written notebooks. It's probably buried in there. But at some point, the software was such that we could keep old terms. I do know that when we changed a term, we would put a *use for*. If we had an old term, we would say *use for* and then show the old term. But it wouldn't document when we did that in the program itself. So that's something that probably should have been done more diligently. But I know; it's in my notes. If I or anybody ever goes through those notes, they might find it. So, there was another part to your question.

Belantara: How did you decide it's time to revise and publish a new edition of the thesaurus? How would you go about making that decision? And then how would you decide on which revisions actually needed to happen?

Castillo-Speed: Okay, so I actually see it a whole different way. It's not like, isn't it time for a new one? It was so organic as part of the indexing process; as we were indexing, we needed to have a new term, so we added a term. And it ended up being put in the thesaurus, in the in-house versions. And then at some point, we printed it on paper and sent it to indexers. That might have been so early that I don't even remember. But more recently, the thesaurus is embedded in the Chicano Database. Major revisions that came out were due to somebody from the outside saying that we should make those changes.

This is where I'll tell the story about my working with Yolanda Retter-Vargas, who was the new head librarian after Richard had left the UCLA Chicano Studies Library. She wasn't the one that came right after him, but in the mid-2000s, she was the librarian there. I started hearing from other people saying, "Yolanda doesn't like the thesaurus. She's going to get in touch with you."

And I'm thinking, "I wonder what that's about."

So finally, she did get in touch with me, and she was concerned about the terms relating to LGBTQ and also the terms that should be in there describing Latinos in the United States and what countries they came from. So, she and I wrote a grant and got some money. We got money from the Librarians Association of the University of California. And it was a grant to revise the thesaurus to add those terms in there.

That was a successful grant. We got two extensions to it. We needed more time, but we did finish, and those were major additions. It wasn't just changing a word here and there. That was like a whole concept that was brought in. That was Yolanda's doing, making that happen.

So, I guess to go back to the original question, I love my work, but there is a lot of it, and I can't spend as much as I want to on the thesaurus and the database. That's the dessert at the end of the day if I can make time. Oh boy, now I get to work on the database! But if I did have more time, I think I would be more conscious about the regular revising of the database or making sure it's okay.

Then the other thing I would like to explain or mention is the fact that the latest version isn't available right now. There is a version available on the Ethnic Studies Libraries website. I had worked with EBSCO, the company that distributes the Chicano Database. Several years ago, we had discussed making the thesaurus available for people who use the database. I pushed back a bit and said we really need to do some more work on it before it gets more public that way. So, in the intervening years, I contracted with a consultant. We did work in two different periods, and we made a lot of great changes, but I haven't had a chance to go back and start over that conversation with EBSCO. For people who have passwords and can get into our maintenance database, there is a list. You can actually see the living list, the living thesaurus. Because of the interest in the thesaurus lately, I've actually figured out that I probably could, with our current programmer, print out that list, even as a PDF, and just have it on the database.

What I'm trying to say is that it does keep changing. If I added a term today then does that mean I send it out as a revised list? I guess I could, now that we can update things more quickly. But in the past, I think it had always been a big chore to think, oh, we're going to have to do a whole project to revise the thesaurus.

Belantara: So, the *Chicano Periodical Index*, CPI for short, drove the need for the thesaurus, and then the Chicano Database came about. Can you talk about how the database actually came to be? And when did you switch from talking about the CPI to just referring to it as the Chicano Database?

Castillo-Speed: When I came on the scene, G.K. Hall had published the first two printed CPI reference books. They are huge books. And then, as I mentioned, the Chicano Studies Library itself published it from the third volume on. I think we went up to a few more volumes after that. That was the printed life of the index. But we started exploring other ways to make the database available to people electronically so that there could be an interface with the data. We published some CD-ROM versions of the database. Once you put it in electronic form, it becomes a database in my mind. We actually had customers, and we were sending them CD-ROM updates for a while, but it was also at a time when, I think, the university became more aware of it through different initiatives.

Richard Chabrán was part of that as well, trying to get the university to be more cognizant of the need to support Chicano and Latino resources at the University of California. He and I were on a committee where the state of California was encouraged to provide some funding to the University of California to enhance Latino collections. One of the things that was recommended was that the CD-ROM of the Chicano Database be distributed to all of the campuses for free—for all campuses to all have it somehow. This recommendation ended up being supported by the University of California administration at a very high level.

Some high-level administrators came to see me one day after that. They introduced me to the idea of having, not just the CD-ROM, but to have it online. They said they could connect me with people at RLG, Research Libraries Group. That was nearby, in the Mountain View, Palo Alto area. With that introduction, I met with RLG and they made it into a file that could be accessible. I can't even remember now what the interface looked like, but it was an interface. Then we had a contract with them and we got royalties from that. So that's when the indexing, I should say the *Chicano Periodical Index*, became the database. It was during that period. We weren't publishing it in print, and we weren't publishing it as a CD-ROM. It became available through this RLG service, and then RLG switched over.

It became an OCLC[5] database. I think it was like RLG was going in a different direction. I think that's what it was. So, its databases became OCLC databases. The same thing happened years later. Select OCLC databases were taken over by EBSCO. So, now our contract is with EBSCO, and EBSCO has its own EBSCO host interface. So that's what people or libraries see when they subscribe to the Chicano Database. That's where the *Chicano Periodical Index* became a database.

Belantara: With all of those transitions between all of these different companies, were you asked about whether or not you still wanted to be working with that company?

Castillo-Speed: Not really. We didn't have much choice. We could go back and say, "Okay, let's create our own product." This has been done by

---

5. OCLC, formerly the Online Computer Library Center, is a cooperative organization that provides services for libraries.

other projects where they made their own interface, they sold their own product, and they weren't part of a bigger company. And we've always kind of had that in mind that that could be like a... I don't how to say it, emergency exit or something because we couldn't rely on businesses. We had a good relationship with RLG, but they had a business decision to make, and we could go along or not go along. We couldn't say, "Oh, why don't we do this instead?"

We weren't part of that at that level. Same thing with OCLC. That was more like, this is a big change. We weren't the only ones that were affected. This was happening to a lot of databases. You can't fight that. I couldn't see how we had a way to fight that. Then, when EBSCO came along, we had a really good relationship with EBSCO at the beginning. We still do, but we did have a lot more person-to-person contact in the past. They came to visit; they came to talk. There were different things that they asked.

They even asked if we could change the name of the database. We didn't do that. I think they wanted something that had Hispanic in it, something like that. They didn't put up a big fight, but they were trying to make it seem more marketable. The name doesn't exactly represent what's in the database because it is Latino and not just Mexican-American experience anymore.

In our advertising we try to tell people, but, for history's sake, we've always kept the name Chicano, and for identity's sake, because that's what it was: the Chicano Database. That was years and years ago. They haven't come back and asked, "You want to change it?"

Over the years working with the different staff persons at EBSCO, I've learned that people change. You have a good relationship with one person, and it's a new person. There's nothing bad about that. It's just that you have to start over again and work with another person. But it's been cordial and friendly and good with the staff persons that I work with. I have not had as much contact with the top people as I did at the beginning. I've seen more of the programmers and their publicity staff. We work a lot with the publicity people. They help us when we go to conferences, and they provide free materials to give out. They're very helpful with that.

Figure 3. The Chicano Database was the first ethnic studies database published on CD-ROM. Castillo-Speed is featured on this brochure that marketed the database.

Drabinski: I'd like to ask about that particular technological shift to the CD-ROM. The Chicano database was the first ethnic studies database to be released on CD-ROM in 1990. Can you say a bit about the decision to move to that technology and what were some of the challenges and benefits?

Castillo-Speed: Again, it's not me by myself; it was Richard and Francisco talking about these things. On my end, I think part of it was like, oh, there's this great new thing, CD-ROM; we don't want to be left behind. We want to be up to date; we want to take advantage of new technology. I think we wanted to be aware of it in case that was something that would be the answer to everything. We also had to figure out the interface because we weren't programmers.

We couldn't just say, "Okay, here's the program to put on CD-ROM and then there it goes." We had to find out how that all worked and how to get experts involved in creating a CD-ROM for the interface part of it. If we wanted to just have all the data there? Okay, maybe that wouldn't be so hard, but the whole point was to be able to send it to somebody, and they would have a CD-ROM reader, and then they'd be wowed. Like, "Oh, look, you can look up all these great things!"

We wanted to be part of this new thing, but we also didn't want to be left behind. Little did I know that the CD-ROM would not last that long. It all changes really fast.

Belantara: So, you already commented on this, but we wanted to learn a little bit more about your decision in 1992 to expand the scope of Chicano Database to include materials related to Puerto Ricans and Central Americans. How was this decision made after it was initially focused on the Mexican-American experience?

Castillo-Speed: It's kind of a no-brainer, but I'm trying to figure out now why it was a no-brainer. Here's one thought that I hadn't really pondered before, but, the project started, and I'm trying to index Chicano movement journals, right? But even at the time that the project started, that outflow of production was already starting to ebb. Chicano journals that published Chicano writers, scholars, and artists, in some cases, lasted forever. The journal *Aztlán*,[6] from UCLA, has lasted all these years. Whereas the one that was published very early on in Berkeley, *El Grito*,[7] is no longer published.

So, when scholars were looking for places to publish and because now there were Chicano Studies programs and Ethnic Studies Departments, they were trying to get published in other places, not in Chicano movement journals. So, a lot of the academic scholarship was being published in places besides Chicano journals. Part of all this was realizing that the original source was not going to last forever. Looking at what

---

6. *Aztlán: A Journal of Chicano Studies*, University of California Press.
7. *El Grito: A Journal of Contemporary Mexican American Thought*, Quinto Sol Publications.

other sources there were, academic journals or other journals or magazines, we didn't really make that distinction. So, we had to open up that anyway. But also, realizing that if we wanted to add more types of materials, like books or articles in books or newspaper articles, then there had to be changes to the database. So, that was working with programmers.

We had another series of programmers, and that's what I worked with them on. Now we're going to try to add fields; that was the basic thing, adding another field. How do you make this a book citation instead of a journal citation? Over the years we worked with programmers to make those changes. Adding books was another way of getting to another source of material. Also, as I mentioned before, more books were being published. I mean, at the beginning, and this goes back to when Francisco was showing me that original collection back in 1983. When I first saw it, he would show me a book and say, "Okay, if people are looking for anything on migration, this is the book. And just think about what that means. This is *the* book."

For Chicanas, I remember that there were probably a handful. Okay, it wasn't just one, but I remember that these are the important ones. And so, he would show me, these are the books on, this is the book or the best book or one of the books on immigration. So now because of Ethnic Studies departments, because of Chicano Studies Programs, people are getting degrees, writing books, getting tenure; they have to get tenure; they have to write books; they have to write articles. So now there are more and more books, whereas, before, you'd have to draw from anthropology or sociology and say, "Well, there's a chapter in here on farm workers." That's why it was in the library in the first place. But that was all there was.

So anyway, what I'm trying to say is that now there is a lot more. So, then we started adding books, and I guess at that point we just thought, look, we don't want to limit ourselves in the future. At one point we even added fields for web links or something trying to anticipate what we would want in the future. So yeah, I think it was more like trying to accommodate where we thought things might go, but also accommodating where the literature was coming out.

Belantara: In the article that we talked about earlier,[8] you mentioned how the *Chicano Thesaurus* was really filling an ethno-specific need, not a language need. Once the database started indexing materials related to other groups, did you also incorporate cultural terms used by people from those communities into the thesaurus?

Castillo-Speed: The first thing we would do probably would be to put in the terms that came up. If they came up over and over again, make them supplementary terms and then see later on. If we're using this all the time, we'd better make it an index term. So they went into this holding, this waiting room stage. Other terms did come up. I have to say, there was a conservative, how should I say it, feeling on my part. I'm like, what can I do? How much time and effort can I put into this? Do we want to expand it and am I the authority on these terms?

So, I think a lot of times it was, mostly, okay, let's hold those terms until they become unavoidable. We have so much literature on this that we have to use it, but it's always there as a supplementary term. And then we try to keep those consistent, so we aren't using a whole lot of different versions of that supplementary term. I don't think we ever did something that I could say was a standard method for doing that. It's more like, as things come up, we react to them.

When I contracted with the lexicographer consultant—wonderful person, wonderful work, and brilliant—the time I spent with her working on this was really well spent. We did make some good changes because I have felt over the years that one of these days I need to go back and look at it over again. I need to make sure that it's presentable. That I could say, yes, this is the latest version, but it's only when working with Kristen, her name's Kristen Jeffries, that I could feel a little bit like I was keeping up. She went back and found some terms that were outdated and no longer used and just negative kinds of things that I should have taken out a long

---

8. Castillo-Speed, L. (1984). "The Usefulness of the *Chicano Thesaurus* for Indexing Chicano Materials." In *Biblio-Politica: Chicano Perspectives on Library Service in the United States*, 169-178. Chicano Studies Publications Unit.

time ago. But it's not that easy to take things out once they're embedded in the database.

One of our earlier versions of the database was on Microsoft Access and that one, and the previous version, the Alpha Micro 1000, were relational databases. So, if you made a change to a term, it automatically changed it in all of the citations. Whereas, what we have now does not do that. That was a drawback when we changed over, but we've had to deal with it a different way. It is more complicated. It isn't that easy to change a term, not just because it's a substitute. If you just had X term and you wanted to substitute Y, if they mean exactly the same thing, then, that can be done through the computer. You could write a simple program. Actually, we have a program now that we can use to do that. But if you're making a change where the term could imply a lot of other concepts in it, and then you use that term instead, then you don't know if a citation might have other terms that would be duplicative of the term that you're trying to add in.

So, you actually do have to look at each one if you're going to do it the right way. You do have to look at them, so that keeps you from wanting to change that term. We have changed some terms, but we really needed to change them. That kind of brings up something I wanted to put on the record here. This is something I learned from Francisco back in the publishing times when we were publishing things; there were books that were being published, not just that reference work, but there were other reference works that came out of the Chicano Studies Library. I was an editorial assistant while I was in library school around that time. Francisco told me, not just me, but our staff; he would say, "If you know something is wrong then you can change it. If you can't change it, okay. But, if you know that it's wrong and you can change it, then fix it."

That stayed with me over the years. So, this whole thing with the thesaurus, I'm not going to put something in there and say, yeah, it's good enough. I want to do it right, but it might take a long time to be done right.

Drabinski: I have another question about the sort of shift to Research Libraries Group and then to EBSCO. Now that the thesaurus is in use in these commercial products, and it's been implemented by the Library of Congress, it feels like it's a mainstream-controlled vocabulary. How do you feel about the sort of mainstream adoption of this work?

Castillo-Speed: First of all, I don't even know if anybody's using it. It was accepted; this was on May 24th, 1990. I got a letter from the Library of Congress, from Sally McCallum, that said they had assigned the code CHT to the thesaurus. The code is to be used in the 6XX subject heading fields. The code was going to be published in part four of *Subject Index Terms: Sources of the US M-A-R-C, US MARC Code List for Relators, Sources, Description Conventions*, when that publication was reissued. It was a short letter.

So that was 1990. We were really, really proud that had happened. We wanted to be recognized. That was great. But over the years, I'm not aware that anybody has been using it. We weren't even using it because that wasn't something that we were able to do. I was asked to come to a meeting at the main library because of that letter; they had wanted to consider whether they could use thesaurus terms. I showed up with a list of terms from the thesaurus that weren't in Melvyl, the UC library catalog at the time. I made copies and passed them out and everything. It was a pleasant meeting, but I don't think they ever actually adopted it. They just said, "Oh, okay, we'll get back to you."

But they considered it; I guess for me it didn't really matter that much either way. Your question implies that maybe it would be, like, absorbed by the mainstream and taken away or something like that. But I was glad about the recognition it got. Really, it exists. Somebody created it, and I'm a career-long member of the American Library Association. So those are important things to me. The Library of Congress is important, ALA is important.

Being a librarian, a professional librarian is important, so to me that was a good recognition. I guess I thought that maybe other people would use it, but if they are using it, I don't know. We haven't heard. Because of the recent webinar I was on, I got contacted by some librarians at UT Austin, I think from the University of Texas. And we had a nice conversation yesterday. And they were asking me if they might use some terms for some newspapers that they're indexing or cataloging. That's my take on it.

THE LIBRARY OF CONGRESS
WASHINGTON, D.C. 20540

NETWORK DEVELOPMENT AND
MARC STANDARDS OFFICE

May 24, 1990

Dear Ms. Castillo-Speed:

Per your letter of May 3, 1990 and your telephone conversation yesterday with Phyllis Bruns of this office, we have assigned the code "cht" to the Chicano Thesaurus for Indexing Chicano Materials found in the Chicano Periodical Index (Berkeley, Chicago Studies Library Publications Unit, University of California, Berkeley). The code is to be used in subfield ǂ2 (Source of heading or term) of 6XX subject heading fields.

Code "cht" will be published in Part IV: Subject/Index Term Sources of the USMARC Code Lists for Relators, Sources, Description Conventions when the publication is reissued.

Sincerely,

Sally H. McCallum
Chief, Network Development and
MARC Standards Office

Ms. Lillian Castillo-Speed
Cicano Studies Library
3404 Dwinelle Hall
University of California, Berkeley
Berkeley, CA 94720

Figure 4. A 1990 letter from Sally H. McCallum from the MARC Standards Office of the Library of Congress shares news that a code was assigned for catalogers to use the Chicano Thesaurus in MARC catalog records

Belantara: So now after all these years, what do you think about the *Chicano Thesaurus* project itself and what would you tell your younger self, Lillian back in 1983 or '84, the year that you took over managing it along with the help of others? You said you always had a team, but what are your thoughts looking back?

Castillo-Speed: Wow, over the years I have felt very grateful that my colleague at library school told me to think about taking this class called Ethnic Bibliography. I might have missed that. I'd have missed the whole thing because I wasn't looking for that at the time when I was in library school.

Being part of this whole project in the broader term of the project, the library, the database, the indexing project, the thesaurus, the network of people, the UCLA and UC Berkeley and all the friendships, all the working together, and just the fact that I had a job almost right out of library school that has lasted until now…there are not many people who can say that.

So, I feel very, very lucky about that. It's something that sustains me and that keeps me going. There's always something new, and this, I guess, might pertain more to being a librarian. It's like every day is another challenge. And I'm just very, very grateful for finding my place, finding something where I felt that I could contribute.

I thought that I was just going to get a library degree, but because of the whole trend towards computer technology, that's what I thought should concentrate on. So, I did concentrate on computers and that combination with then finding out what I could apply that to and how important that was. And of course, learning about myself, my identity, being Chicana myself, learning to even call myself Chicana, at that time, I just felt very lucky about being part of all that.

Belantara: What is your hope for the thesaurus and the database moving forward?

Castillo-Speed: Of course, I hope it continues forever, but I've had to take a longer, more practical view of it. Not just me, but Richard. We're not just working on this. We're working on other things and we see them as important and want to keep working on them. Of course, I'm going to retire sometime or somehow leave. Before COVID hit, I was actually making some long-term plans. Not immediate plans, but like longer term plans to phase out. I mean, to phase somebody in, to take over what I was doing. And so, I met with my supervisor at the time and I was asking like, "How's the budget? If I leave, would I be replaced?"

And at the time they said, "Oh yes, yes, yes."

So that made me feel good at that time, but things have changed now because of COVID. I couldn't leave while all that was going on. I guess what I'm trying to say is that, ideally, I would leave when I knew that I was going to be replaced and ideally I would be part of finding the person. Ideally there would be a person who was willing to be committed to continuing what we have been working on. But I understand on a practical basis that people will find their own things that they are passionate about, and this might not be that.

So, I would like to be involved as an indexer for as long as I can. I see myself as doing that. I'm going to index, then I'll actually have the time to do the stuff I wanted to do every day. I want to do some more indexing, but I don't have the time. If I had the time, that's what I would be doing. I can't keep things from changing. I can't predict the future. But that's what I'd like to think—that at least that one person beyond me would continue working on it.

Belantara: Is there anything else that you would like to add or something that we should have asked you about and didn't get to this time round?

Castillo-Speed: I just do want to emphasize there are other librarians that have been supportive, and people I've mentored even that are part of a group that we have. There are other projects that we're working on. I'm just very, very grateful for that. Whoever is learning about the *Chicano Thesaurus* and the Chicano Database, I hope that they know that it's not one person, it couldn't have been done with just one person. It had to be a group effort.

The Women's Thesaurus

Introduction

The *Women's Thesaurus* was created to provide useful and relevant search terms for the study of women's history, culture, and experience. The vocabulary took shape in the context of feminist activism that located progress in policy work, activism, and scholarship. The project grew out of two distinct efforts. The first was the establishment and promotion of academic women's research centers formed to collect women's magazines, newspapers, and other ephemera that had long been excluded from mainstream libraries. The centers also sought to provide resources to support the burgeoning fields of women's history and women's studies, a growing activist movement, and policymakers who relied on research to inform legislative work. In 1981, thirty-five research centers at academic institutions across the United States came together as the National Council for Research on Women (NCRW) in order to facilitate connection and collaboration among feminist scholars and activists. Some of the participants included Stanford University, the University of Texas, Harvard University, and Wellesley College.

As scholars, policymakers, and activists began writing and publishing their work, they had an acute need for access tools. In order to build on the burgeoning scholarship around women's issues, researchers needed a way to retrieve materials that were obscured by the lack of relevant terms in existing systems. Without robust subject language, women faced significant barriers to accessing feminist literature. In October 1982, Mary Ellen Capek, working under the auspices of the NCRW, convened a Thesaurus Task Force to address this need. Simultaneously, a group of feminist librarians organized an ad hoc Women's Studies Database Task Force within the American Library Association (ALA) to assess existing vocabularies and their usefulness for research about women. The need for access tools was shared by librarians, researchers, and writers alike. The group was charged with investigating the coverage of women's topics in library databases and the usefulness of existing search vocabularies; they published a report on the task force's work two years later. Their research confirmed that existing subject language was insufficient for research into the condition of women, noting that "neither the abstracts or the index terms adequately reflected the content" (Pritchard, 1984, p. x). Many terms did not exist at all, and those that did often failed to capture feminist perspectives on particular topics or reflected patriarchal conceptions of women's experience. Three librarians from that task force, Sarah Pritchard (Library of Congress), Sue Searing (University of Wisconsin), and Pat King (Radcliffe College), joined Capek in her work on the Women's Thesaurus Task Force.

Over the subsequent two years, scholars, activists, and librarians worked collaboratively to develop a set of terms that would enable access to the growing collection of materials in women's centers. Center directors went through their files one-by-one, listing terms that were missing from existing vocabularies but were essential to research on women, such as: *Domestic violence, Sexual harassment, Clitoridectomy,* etc. With financial support from the Ford Foundation and others, the Women's Thesaurus Task Force assembled, collected, iterated, and revised lists of terms into the single volume *A Women's Thesaurus: An Index of Language Used to Describe and Locate Information by and about Women*, published by Harper & Row in 1987 and referred to herein by its shortened title, the *Women's Thesaurus*. The *Ways of Knowing Oral History Project* presents the history of this book through the stories of Mary Ellen Capek, the coordinator and editor of the *Women's Thesaurus*, and Sarah M. Pritchard, a librarian whose involvement in ALA's Task Force led to her to connect with Capek and collaborate on the *Women's Thesaurus*.

Women's Thesaurus Timeline - Milestones

1975
The Business and Professional Women's Foundation discusses need for a shared vocabulary.

1975
The Women's Information Services Network is formed with a major objective to create a cooperative bibliographic database to index research on women and girls.

1976
The Women's Educational Equity Communications Network is formed and begins indexing citations.

1981
The National Council for Research on Women is formed.

1982
American Library Association's Women's Studies Database Task Force is formed.

1982
The Women's Thesaurus Task Force is formed at a National Council for Research on Women meeting. Mary Ellen Capek serves as the project coordinator.

1983
Women's centers type out and send their subject lists to be compiled by Inter-America.

1984 / 1985
Capek and the task force partner with subject matter experts to refine and structure the vocabulary.

1987

The *Women's Thesaurus* is published by Harper & Row.

1989

The *Women's Thesaurus* is assigned the code "wot" by the MARC standards office to be used in subfield 2 of 6XX MARC subject heading fields.

Mary Ellen Capek on the Women's Thesaurus

Biography

Mary Ellen Capek is an organizational researcher and consultant, currently principal of Capek Consulting (www.capekconsulting.com). She is co-author of *Effective Philanthropy: Organizational Success through Deep Diversity and Gender Equality* (The MIT Press, 2006)—launched and funded by the W.K. Kellogg Foundation—which won the 2007 Independent Sector/ARNOVA Virginia A. Hodgkinson Research Prize for the best book on philanthropy in the nonprofit sector that informs policy and practice.

A founding officer of the National Council for Research on Women, a 35-year-old coalition of 120 research and policy centers that merged in 2016 with the International Center for Research on Women, Mary Ellen served as NCRW executive director from 1989 to 1996 and edited *A Women's Thesaurus*, named to *Library Journal's* Best Reference Books 1987 list. From 1975-1983 she served as Associate Director and then Director of Continuing Education at Princeton University, and from 1969-1974 she was a teacher (tenured in 1972) at Essex County College in Newark, NJ. She wrote a well-received textbook, *Writing in Context* (Harcourt Brace Jovanovich, 1976) based on her teaching in Newark.

She has served on numerous boards and committees, including the Aspen Institute's Nonprofit Sector Research Fund, the Independent Sector Research Committee, The Conference Board Work/Life Leadership Council, Funders for Lesbian and Gay Issues, and Equality New Mexico.

Since 2011, she has served as publisher of Arbor Farm Press, a press she helped to launch in 2010 (www.arborfarmpress.com). Mary Ellen's papers are archived at the Schlesinger Library, Radcliffe (NCRW-related publications, speeches, and correspondence); the Rockefeller Archive Center (the Rockefeller Brother Fund research, *locked for twenty years*); Indiana University/Purdue University Indianapolis Library (women in philanthropy/diversity in philanthropy research, speeches, correspondence and notes); the University of Denver (women in higher education research and materials); and the Hilda Raz Archives at the University of Nebraska-Lincoln (poetry).

About the Interview

The following transcribed interview of Mary Ellen Capek took place on July 26, 2022, as part of the *Ways of Knowing Oral History Project*. The interview was auto transcribed and then edited by Amanda Belantara. Care was taken to not alter the original transcription's contents. However, the editors have formatted the following to improve readability and provided footnotes for clarity where appropriate. The original transcript and recording can be accessed through the *Ways of Knowing Oral History Project* held at NYU Libraries.[1]

---

1. Capek's recording is available here: https://search.library.nyu.edu/permalink/01NYU_INST/1d6v258/alma990098389950107871.

Transcript from the *Ways of Knowing Oral History Project*

Interviewee: Mary Ellen Capek, Editor, The *Women's Thesaurus*
Interviewers: Amanda Belantara
Date: July 26, 2022
Location: Virtual Interview; Corrales, New Mexico

Amanda Belantara: Today, we're interviewing Mary Ellen Capek, editor and coordinator of the Women's Thesaurus Task Force. The interview was conducted for the *Ways of Knowing Oral History Project*. The interview took place virtually on July 26th, 2022, recorded locally by Hannah Crawford at Mary Ellen's home in Corrales, New Mexico. The interviewer is Amanda Belantara, based in New York City. Mary Ellen, I'd like to start off today's interview by just learning a little bit more about your background and education?

Mary Ellen Capek: Oh my! Well, I started out with a PhD in Contemporary Poetry, and my first teaching job, because there were very few the year I finished, was in Newark, New Jersey, right after the riots,[2] and a community college, Essex County College, had just formed the year before. So, I was in a position as a newly minted PhD, teaching poetry to mostly Black and Hispanic adults, many of whom had a very low level of education because of Newark Public Schools. And by the end of that time, with my teaching in Newark, which was an amazing experience, I learned a lot more than they did, I realized how much language influenced so much of their lives, and by being able to get them more confident in their own language and finding their language...

This was also the era when Black language was first starting to get acknowledged, and Spanglish was another version that we dealt with. I learned a lot about the power of language in people's lives. I had studied some linguistics as a graduate student and was very interested in all of that. I went from there to Princeton, running the Continuing Education

---

2. On July 12, 1967, two white police officers, John DeSimone and Vito Pontrelli, assaulted John Smith, a Black cab driver, following a traffic stop. In response, members of the Black community rose up in protest of ongoing police brutality. The armed conflict ended on July 17 after multiple deaths, injuries, and arrests.

Program, which was crazymaking in the sense that I dealt with organizational issues that were way beyond anything I'd ever experienced before. And that process very quickly led me, for sanity reasons, to working with a group called the American Council on Education's National Identification Program for the Advancement of Women in Higher Education Administration, which we abbreviated as ACENIP.

That program was really important to the thesaurus because we got some funding through somebody I had met at the Ford Foundation through that project. We also got funding from the Prudential Foundation, which became one of the supporters of the thesaurus because they really liked what we were trying to do. A lot of that work led to my being included, because of the grant funding from Ford, into the coalition that first created the National Council for Research on Women. So, all of that was a very circumlocutious world, but it led to my being part of the Council. I saw that as an incredible opportunity for doing something really important and necessary. This was 1980 and 1981. We needed to, basically, pool together the existing centers for research on women, many of which had been funded by the Ford Foundation. It was really a needed coalition, because there were policy folks and activist groups, as well as the basic research centers like Rutgers, Stanford, Wellesley, several at Harvard and Radcliffe, and those centers were putting out amazing research and all kinds of important policy analyses.

Belantara: You mentioned the Council, so I just want to take a step back for a second, and could you tell us what the National Council for Research on Women was and how it was formed?

Capek: It merged with an International Center for Research on Women, I guess, about four or five years ago, but it kept going for a good thirty-five years. And basically, it was a coalition, initially, of centers that had been funded by the Ford Foundation.

Belantara: And when you say centers, could you elaborate? What type of centers?

Capek: Research centers. The Wellesley Center for Research on Women, Stanford Center for Research on Women, policy centers in Washington, Business and Professional Women's Foundation. A lot of these centers then joined together and started to find curiosity in each other. A lot of my interest in this from the get-go was working to bridge research, policy and practice because, as you might expect, the research centers were used to talking to other researchers, the policy centers preferred policy, and the activists didn't much like any of them, other than other activists. I remember one of our very early meetings, one of the policy people hurled a bunch of three-by-five index cards into the audience and said, "Until you girls learn to put your research on these cards, forget about it!"

So there was a lot of antipathy among the various perspectives. But it was important because the vision there was really to transform how the world thought about women and girls. I mean, it was not that we lacked ambition. And we did work, from the very beginning, with some international centers, but mostly, it was a national coalition initially. And it's wonderful that we ended up with the international coalitions, but initially, there was just a lot of interest in bringing together these centers so they could learn from each other.

A lot of new ideas were really fomenting then, thinking race, gender and class, for example, not studying in isolation, in silos, but really trying to bridge into wider understanding. At least my vision, and a few other people, we had the notion of trying to connect up using technology. That was way before, obviously, we had the Internet and email was common. I was at Princeton, so I had access to ARPAnet and some of the other more current technologies. We had a connection to the educational testing service in Princeton, which donated email addresses to all of our center directors back then. I think we had twenty-nine, to answer your earlier question, in the beginning.

Belantara: Twenty-nine centers were members of the National Council for Research on Women?

Capek: And we went from twenty-nine; eventually we were close to 120, 130, I don't have the exact numbers in my head.

Belantara: Were you co-director of the Council?

Capek: No, I started out as executive secretary, which meant I took the minutes, which is one of the more powerful positions in any organization. I was very clear from the beginning that I wanted this to bridge research, policy, and practice. Not everybody was so enthusiastic about that. And because I got to take the minutes, whenever I got a chance, I would write in [the words] "research, policy, and practice."

And sooner or later that mantra got so that it was quite comfortable for most people there, but it did become a really strong sense of possibility of bridging these gaps among us. One of the things, though, that was funny, that I think should be pointed out, was that this experiment we had with email, initially, was a complete bust. We started out giving everybody email addresses and encouraging them to share their ideas and thoughts, and nowadays, it just seems bizarre to think there were days when we couldn't do that. But it was amazing because I learned two things from that experiment: that people had to have something to say, and they needed to say it regularly.

They needed to log on every day, and for the most part, people didn't want to do that. So, we put that on the shelf, waiting until the technology caught up with the folks in the centers, and it eventually did. But I also remembered a board meeting, standing up on a table at one point and throwing a phone book around in front of a microphone and said, "This, ladies, this is a database."

Because there was a lot of fear of technology among a lot of those folks.

Belantara: So before, you mentioned a couple of these other organizations, and I just wanted to clarify, what was the relationship between the National Council for Research on Women, the Business and Professional Women's Foundation and the Women's Educational Equity Communications Network? And you weren't involved in all of them, but they all played a role in the Council, is that correct?

Capek: The Business and Professional Women's Foundation was an organization that became a member center of the Council. And they were incredibly instrumental in getting this thesaurus project off the ground. It wouldn't have happened without them. The librarian there [Cheryl Sloan] was a force of nature. She was excellent. She's the one that first found Inter-America [Research Associates], which was a research group in DC.

They were interested in getting their own collection online and accessible, which was their motivation for doing it. But there was a group earlier in 1975; they had a meeting, I think it was at Wellesley, bringing together maybe fifteen or so centers, almost all of whom became members of the Council eventually, talking about the need for this, and nothing happened from it that I know. It was an important meeting; it got the idea through to some people, but nothing really happened until the Council itself formed. The other group that you mentioned, I think, was a product of a grant, some federal funding that was available. To the best of my knowledge, we didn't work closely with them.

My memory, which, obviously this was a long time ago, my memory is that most of the people that had been involved in earlier iterations of these needs joined the work we were doing. And a lot of what my skillset was back then was collaboration, was getting different groups who really didn't much like working together to actually enjoy each other and do it. We used to have some wonderful annual meetings because we would ask a lot of dumb questions, or I would, and it really got people thinking and out of their usual jargon from their disciplines, so we actually got people much more engaged.

But it wasn't until we had... Oh, I guess it was like the second year of the Council, we had a meeting, we were sitting around talking, and one of the biggest problems that was identified was that these centers had all of this incredible, groundbreaking research of all kinds, and there was very little way to access it. Most of it would've been deemed by you librarians as ephemeral. A lot of it was published, or if it was published in more traditional journals, political science journals, law journals, social science journals, it wouldn't have been able to be accessed, because the language of those existing databases didn't contain any of the language that we needed to describe the work. We really looked at it and said, "This is a huge problem, and we have got to address it, and we have to address it with some imagination and curiosity."

I don't think I was running the meeting, I think I was just a participant, and when I heard all of that, I just got so excited, because that was like my dream job. I was very influenced, as a graduate student, by Adrienne Rich.[3] Her *Dream of a Common Language*[4] was like lightning going off in my head when I read that book. It was like, "Here's somebody that understands we don't have words for the worlds that we're experiencing, for the life that we're trying to lead. We don't have language for it."

And I love the title of this project, Ways of Knowing, because that was, really, what we were up against. There weren't very many of them back then. And for me at least, this was an attempt, in a very prosaic way, to take Adrienne's *Dream of a Common Language* and put it into practice. And very quickly, we connected with the librarian groups. The ALA had a good working group that was very involved in all of this. They understood the issues, but they themselves hadn't had much of a chance. Because of their own work responsibilities, they didn't have the opportunity to pull it together, so that's something I knew how to do.

Belantara: Could you just, in your own words, tell us about the *Women's Thesaurus* and its goals?

Capek: Whoa! Well, the goals, initially, were to open up the existing thesauri out there, the databases that were clueless, that didn't even have language like domestic violence or sexual harassment in their thesauri. Another goal was to transform the Library of Congress's subject headings and the other systems of cataloging that are out there. That's why I was so grateful for the librarians we had working with us.

---

3. Adrienne Rich was a white lesbian poet, essayist, and feminist activist.
4. Rich, Adrienne, *The Dream of a Common Language*. New York: Norton, 1978.

The three that were most closely involved as part of the steering committee, were Pat King, from the Schlesinger Library at Radcliffe; Sue Searing, who, at that point, was the University of Wisconsin Women's Studies librarian; and Sarah Pritchard, who was a Library of Congress librarian. And those three were amazing allies in all of this. They had the skillsets that I didn't. They could provide the technical knowledge. I didn't have a clue. I mean, I thought thesaurus, when we first started this, was *Roget*, right?[5] That it was a technical term that was used to describe all these displays, the alphabetical display, the hierarchical display, the rotated... I mean, I didn't have any idea what that was when we first started this. All I knew was that we had access to a lot of very important language. And to pull that together initially, we just grabbed lists of language from all the file cabinets in our centers.

The goal was not to give them a whole new language. They would never have used it. These are mostly guys and they're mostly arrogant and they're mostly convinced they have the handle around the world that they know and understand and articulate. And what we were trying to do was say, "whoa guys, wait a minute. We have a few other pieces of reality we want you to look at."

Belantara: You explained in the introduction that the goal was never to replace the existing classification systems but, instead, to ensure compatibility with them. Could you tell us a little bit more about this?

Capek: We were very pragmatic, at least I was, and a lot of the people I was working with were, because what we were trying to do was transform the existing systems. Those systems were the ones used by most

---

5. *Roget's Thesaurus* is a popular English-language thesaurus understood widely as a source for synonyms.

people, certainly in academia and in policy analysis and in activism. So, you've got systems, especially in the traditional social sciences and natural sciences, even, and literature.

The goal was not to give them a whole new language. They would never have used it. These are mostly guys and they're mostly arrogant, and they're mostly convinced they have the handle on the world that they know and understand and articulate. And what we were trying to do was say, "Whoa, whoa, whoa, whoa, whoa guys, wait a minute. We have a few other pieces of reality we want you to look at, and here are a couple: Domestic violence, sexual harassment..." Like that. I don't ever remember even conversations about doing this as our own unique system. It was always trying to transform the existing systems.

Belantara: You just were sort of talking about this right now, but I wonder if you could elaborate a little bit further because, in your article "Wired words," you wrote, "As a reference tool, the thesaurus is designed to lead users into the language, to broaden awareness of other ways in which language structures our thinking."[6]

Capek: Yes.

Belantara: Can you talk more about that?

Capek: I sure can.

One of the things that just recently came to my knowledge was not just the thesaurus, as the tool that we were just talking about, transforming the existing access sources, it was also giving centers a way of organizing their own filing that was compatible with other centers. So, it was a way of making the language more mutually useful with each other. But it turns out the thesaurus is a mental health issue, you know?

I'll give you the example that I just got hold of. Hilda Raz, who was one of three women editors of a national literary magazine, *The Prairie*

---

6. Capek, M.E.S., "Wired Words: Developing an Online Thesaurus and Database for Improving Access to Women's Information Resources," *Women and Language*, 10, no. 1 (1986): 54.

Schooner, received a copy of the thesaurus as a review book. Well, in Hilda's case, she had said that this is not the kind of book they usually reviewed. They tended to review poetry, novels, short stories... literature, basically. But she saw this and immediately claimed dibs on it, if you know that expression, "I got dibs on that."

So okay, Hilda got dibs on that, and it went in her office, not outside. And she talked about it in graduate seminars, and the graduate students started being curious, coming into her office to use it. But Hilda said she used to use it because she would get very discouraged by all the sexism she was up against, and that she, one day, went into her office and shut the door and just started browsing. And she laughed and laughed and laughed.

And she said ever since that one time, she did that regularly. Whenever she got depressed or overwhelmed, she would just go in and read it. And I just absolutely loved that story. I had no idea how people were using it.

Belantara: How did you first become interested or involved in working on the Women's Thesaurus Task Force? Can you remember who originally suggested the project?

Capek: I cannot. The group, it would've been, you know, pretty much the Council's board; it might well have been a board meeting. It was certainly a group of women directors of our centers who had identified the problem. I mean, period, the problem was not getting the materials and the resources out there so folks could use it. But I saw immediately in a much broader context that this was not just that—it was transforming the language.

This was Adrienne Rich writ large. This was my chance to take Adrienne Rich and the poetry that I had loved and, actually, as homage to Rich, end up giving her a volume of our language. And I still get goosebumps and my eyes tear up sometimes when I think about that because the damn thing came out thicker than Julia Child's work at the time!

And it was very much what we had hoped for, what I had hoped for. The first three or four years were simply iterations. We would pull lists of the language from file cabinets, and we would compile them. Cheryl Sloan, the librarian at the B & PW Foundation had Inter-America, I think it was, that she had found that would combine the lists, put them together, and we'd send them back out.

Belantara: And so, before we go into that, I just wanted to back up for a moment. And so, you were at a Council meeting, and then this project came about and you decided this was your dream job. So then, after you decided to take this on, how did the task force actually form, and how were members selected?

And then, a second part of that question would be, how do you feel the group's composition, in terms of race, class, and geographic location may have impacted the thesaurus?

Capek: I think what we basically did was to build off of volunteers. I mean, it wasn't like we went out and recruited people. I tried in a few cases, where I knew we didn't have the librarians we needed. I think I was the one that found Sarah Pritchard, but I'm not even sure of that.

Belantara: Were the volunteers all members of the Council, or how did you go about identifying potential volunteers?

Capek: Well, very early on, I think it might have been Pat King, who was the head of the Schlesinger Library at Radcliffe. She might have put us in touch with the ALA librarians task force on women's stuff,[7] and once we hooked up with Sarah and with Sue Searing, it was smooth sailing from there, that they knew other librarians they could pull in. Everybody knew somebody that was interested in this project. So, to the best of my knowledge, people pretty much volunteered for the Women's Thesaurus Task Force.

---

7. The Feminist Task Force was established in 1970 as part of ALA's Social Responsibilities Round Table, seeking to address ongoing issues of sexism in American libraries. The group continues to the present day.

Belantara: And can you remember roughly how many people were actually part of the task force?

Capek: I think it was about twenty, maybe a little bit, a few more. I think we tried really hard to get as much representation as we could, certainly around race issues. We were trying that from the very beginning. And Council members went out of our way to make sure we had at least some balance of race on the board, the very first board we had. And I think we made a commitment; I know I did, and I think other people on the board made a similar commitment to doing that. And it was very important that we do that.

Cheryl Sloan herself was Black, and she, very much, was instrumental in how we approached the first round of this stuff. I know, once we got into the subject groups, that was one of the mandates they were given: "What is the language in your field, and make sure you reach out to a variety of different folks that care about this, not just your regular white gals." So, we were pretty aware of all of that when we got started.

Belantara: And how frequently did the task force meet? And how would members correspond?

Capek: I don't remember. I mean, we didn't meet that often, and it was mostly phone interactions, mailing... I mean, I remember getting from Cheryl the first batch of integrated lists when we did the lists for the very first time from our centers. We pulled those together and we sent them back. So that would've been, you know, snail mail. It was, like, you know, put the postage on and send it. And I remember having phone conversations... This would've been 1982, 1983, you know, there wasn't a lot of opportunity to do more than regular old mail and telephone stuff. It seems like the Dark Ages, in retrospect.

Belantara: You've got the task force; you're coordinating everybody's work. Tell us about how this work actually got started. Where, when, and how did it happen, and how did you go about coordinating the group and dividing the labor?

Capek: What I remember is that, from the beginning I was the one committed to making this happen, and I knew it was going to take a long time, and I knew it was going to take a lot of collaboration. And I did know, by then, how to do collaboration because I'd run a statewide coalition network that brought in as many different voices as possible, and it didn't unnerve me. I appreciated it and enjoyed it, so I was absolutely committed to making this whole thing take off. And I knew some of the initial work that had to happen, which was getting other people excited about it. And they were.

It didn't take a lot to get people excited about it. What it took was patience, which is not my strong suit. And a lot of the time, it was just following up with phone calls, saying, "Did you get the second list yet? No, well, give me a deadline. When can you get it back to us?"

So, there was a little bit of nagging involved, I expect, but I'm not even sure. The word I used earlier was iteration, and that's really what it was. It was an iterative process. We must have gone back to everybody three or four or five times. And every time you did it, you thought of more and more and more and more and more words. So, it was just, like, it grew and it grew and it grew. It was like yeast!

The whole thing expanded, and it kept expanding and it kept expanding. So, you know, once we got closer to the fifth iteration of all of these lists, it was clear we had to do something to make it more manageable, because no one person, me included, could wrap our heads around all of this as a draft. So late one night, I came home and I thought, "We have got to have subject groups." And it was this moment of power. I carved the universe into eleven groups, and it was so... I mean, I didn't do it by myself. I did a draft and then I sent it to everybody, and everybody else weighed in, and then everybody else weighed in again. And it took a couple of iterations, but we did come up with a draft of eleven chunks that we slotted things into. We needed that for the thesaurus itself because it has a subject display.

Belantara: You've got everybody onboard; you're the catalyst, so to speak, keeping everybody motivated. How did you secure funding for this project? You've mentioned already in the interview a couple of different sponsors like Ford Foundation, but how did your group actually solicit sponsorship from these corporations, and were the funders involved at all beyond providing financial support?

Capek: Not really. It wasn't that hard because other funders... I mean, we had the core funding from Ford, that was the coalition, our Council, that we really were a product of the Ford Foundation. Even as we added more centers that didn't have Ford funding, we still felt Ford was, you know, our daddy—or mommy—as the case may be. But back then, at least, we got core support from Ford to keep us going. They really cared about trying to do this as a coalition, not just as the thesaurus, the project itself, of the Council, because they saw it as maximizing their own dollars. With that kind of collaboration, it was what philanthropy calls a multiplier effect. And so, Ford was happy that we were doing this, but we also had core support that I had brought from Prudential that had funded my work in Princeton initially, and we got some core support from the Lilly Foundation.

Those three were really the core. And then, there's a whole list of others. I can read them off if you want me to do that for the record, listed in the Thesaurus: Aetna Life and Casualty, Atlantic Richfield, Chevron, Levi Strauss Foundation, Mobile, PerkinElmer Corporation, Prudential, Sears Roebuck, Sophia Fund, Tandy Corporation, Texas Philanthropic Foundation, and the Xerox Foundation.

Belantara: That's amazing that the Council was able to garner support from all of those different organizations. Were you the one involved directly?

Capek: To some extent, yes. I could talk a good game. Very early on I learned to be a good fundraiser. Our president of the Council back then had been a program officer at the Ford Foundation, and she was very good at fundraising too, although she tended to mostly go back to Ford for the money. So, it was much more me reaching out to a lot of different sources and some of our member centers doing that work also. I know Pat King from the Schlesinger was really helpful with trying to get funding. The other librarians were as well. So, we really got a lot of help from a lot of different people.

Once this started to shape up, folks really saw the need for it and the usefulness of it. And especially for foundations. My work after the Council was in philanthropy. I did another whole round of work as a researcher and consultant in philanthropy. And one of the things we know about foundations is that they like to see a lot of bang for their buck, especially if it's safe.

And in this case, the *Women's Thesaurus* was seen as an intellectual project, a project with immediate application, as well as safe, so to speak. And that may be putting the wrong cast on it for some folks, but it was a project that I think people appreciated, and it wasn't that hard to raise money for it, quite frankly. And the Council itself ended up donating at least a year of my time. And then, eventually, toward the end when we were doing editing full-time, I got a sabbatical of six months to do the editing.

Belantara: What were some of the learning curves for you, both individually and for the group? And when you decided to take this project on, what were some of your first steps?

Capek: Well, as I said earlier, for me it was an incredible opportunity. If I could have designed my dream job, this would've been it. Because A) it's working with language, which I love, and B) it's a philosophical and political issue for me, trying to find language to describe the worlds that we experience. And, as I said earlier, Adrienne Rich and some of the other poets: Mary Daly, Audre Lorde, others. Well, Mary Daly's not a poet, but some of her work certainly spoke to the need to come up with a different frame of reference than what we were stuck with—with this, you know, white male stream of language.

And what I had learned in Newark was how important language was in isolating people. You could create ghettos simply by not allowing folks into the access of the language that they used. In fact, I'm in the middle of writing my last book called *The Power of Naming*, because this is a whole project that has stuck with me like glue through the whole of my life. It's essential how much language needs to be opened up. So, I saw this from the get-go as something that was hugely important—not just to me, but to scholarship in general, to the political world in general, and eventually to women's lives. And I think pretty much everybody on that task force shared a similar vision.

I didn't need to explain it. Everybody got it.

Belantara: These are all really inspiring ideas, and it sounds like you were highly motivated and connected to this topic but, from a practical perspective, what did you do? When you just said, "Okay, I've agreed to take on this project, what do I do now?" What were some of the first things that you did?

Capek: Very first thing was getting our centers to share their file headings. I mean, it sounds simplistic, but it was essential because they were the source of the language we wanted to get hold of.

Belantara: Your article mentions that terms from thirty-five research centers, libraries, publishers, and associations were collected to help inform the thesaurus.[8] So, how did you identify and select these? And how did they extract and then provide their list to the task force?

Capek: It's pretty straightforward. I mean, it sounds absurdly simple, but simply going through file cabinets, literally pulling out the drawers from A to E, and writing down the subject headings of the files.

---

8. Capek, M.E.S., "Wired Words: Developing an Online Thesaurus and Database for Improving Access to Women's Information Resources," *Women and Language*, 10, no. 1 (1986): 54.

Belantara: But you have thirty-five research centers and so for each center, somebody working there is opening all of their file drawers, taking note of every single heading?

Capek: Yep.

Belantara: Can you describe, step by step, what it would look like in order to get that to you?

Capek: Well, I'm sure they put it in a computer. We did have computers back then. When I started out, I wasn't going to do this work, I said, unless I got my, you know, back then it was an IBM PC, and so we did have computers. Most of the centers had at least one computer, and I'm sure they would've typed all of this into the computer, printed them out, and mailed it to me. And then we, in turn, sent those to Washington where Cheryl submitted them to Inter-America, which merged the lists. They were a research organization. I don't know the extent to which they were a library-based organization, but they were definitely a research and development group, and they had enough computer capacity to take those individual lists. I mean, this was before we really had fancy spreadsheets.

Nowadays, you'd just pull them into, you know, either a Word file or a spreadsheet, and interlink them, but you couldn't do that back then. Cheryl would get that group to produce the linked files and then we'd send it back again. That's where the iterative process started. I mean, it's really very boring in some ways.

Belantara: It's exciting to me to hear all this collective effort that is behind the thesaurus.

Capek: Well, and once you got those lists, what was so interesting was that it would spark more words. I'm sure, I don't remember specifically, but I'm sure for the second or third iteration of those lists going back to the centers that had contributed in the first place, they would think, "Oh yeah, that reminds me. There's this, and there's this word and there's this word."

So basically, it was a trigger for adding more language to those lists. And that's really how the whole thing got built, initially.

Belantara: And so there were thirty-five places that you gathered the headings from. How did you identify them, because I imagine there may have been more than thirty-five around the country at the time. Did you actually have different centers that you definitely wanted to include specifically? Or any whose terms kind of stood out, and maybe had a predominant impact on the task force's work?

Capek: What I remember about that is that, initially, we went with any of the member centers that wanted to be part of this. We gave everybody the option of joining this, or at least of submitting their language. And, you know, a few didn't, but, you know, I think we had a pretty good representation just from the Council member centers.

Belantara: You already talked a little bit about combining these lists, you went with the company. Could you talk a little bit more about the process then?

Capek: You know, it's interesting because I don't have access to the archives anymore. I was sort of kicking myself. I would love to have poked around back there. They're all at the Schlesinger Library, up at Radcliffe, the archives. And it would be fascinating to be able to go back and plow through some of that. But, as best I recall, what we did was just really keep this back and forth going.

Belantara: And the back and forth, that's all using snail mail, is that right?

Capek: Yes. All snail, yes, right.

Belantara: So how thick was the initial combined list? And you would send that same list out to each person on the task force? And then, would you talk on a conference call to get everybody's input? Or would you, as coordinator, talk to each person or each group?

Capek: I don't remember specifically. I think pretty much what we did was ask people to go through the list and add stuff that was missing. And then we took those combined lists and got still another clean printout. But it was when we switched to the subject groups, that's what really made the difference, and made it much easier and much—I shouldn't say easier—made it much more in-depth, because once people could get into their own areas, we could then divide some of the responsibility.

Each of the subject groups had a person who was in charge, and they took responsibility for reaching out to others in the subject group, as well as others that weren't, to take their language and say, "Okay, which of these terms on this combined list belong in our subject group and which ones are missing?"

So, once we started pulling those into subject groups, holes emerged, and we saw more clearly where we needed to add more expertise or add more words, add more expertise so we could add more words, and it just sort of grew from there. Yeah.

Belantara: And so, are these the eleven categories that eventually structured the thesaurus that you're talking about?

Capek: Yes.

Belantara: The subject specialties—let's go back to that moment that you shared a bit earlier, when you said that you had this revelatory moment where you got to divide the universe. So how did you actually make that decision initially? And then, how did you decide upon each of the eleven categories?

Capek: It was me sitting down at night thinking we've got to carve this up so it's manageable. What are the most salient groups that make sense for both the research that we've got in our centers and for the reality of the universe we're working in. And so, I just pulled them together.

I mean, it wasn't rocket science, it was just sitting down and saying, "How do we divide it up?" It's not complicated, it really is not. And it surprised me how easy it was to become a commander of the universe before you even started.

Belantara: So, was it your executive decision? Or was that something that the task force decided collectively? You came up with all the categories, is that correct?

Once we got closer to the fifth iteration of all of these [word] lists, it was clear we had to do something to make it more manageable, because no one person, me included, could wrap our heads around all of this as a draft. So late one night, I came home and I thought, "We have got to have subject groups." And it was this moment of power. I carved the universe into eleven groups…

Capek: I did initially, but then, the way we were working was very collaborative, so I sent them around to everybody again. "So hey, guys, look, this is what I came up with late last night with a stiff bourbon. What are you doing about this? Do you agree? Are there things I've missed? Does this capture the universe that we are trying to capture?"

You know, what's missing? And you know, I don't remember how much change they actually made. There wasn't a lot. They maybe combined a few, renamed a few, like history and social change, I remember, that got refined. *Government law, Government, Public policy,* they combined those together. I think I had *Law* separately at one point. So, stuff like that.

Belantara: What do you think about these categories today?

Capek: You know, I don't really think much about them. I think they still work. There would be more focus, maybe trying to put within each category, race, class, and gender, make that more specific. But these really are sort of the basic spread of knowledge in the way most groupings work. I mean, we're dealing more, not with academia per se, because we were trying to bring in policy and activism, but, you know, we don't have research here. *Science and technology* would include engineering, for example. That wasn't made specific back then. So, there are gaps.

Again, one of the things I always knew as a linguistics student in graduate school, and it's certainly proven true over the years, is that language is a living, organic entity. It's not something that's ever fixed. And what we were trying to do with the thesaurus project was basically doing a fix in time. Trying to say, "Okay, here's a snapshot. In 1987, this is what our world, as women researchers, policy specialists and activists, looks like. These are the words that describe our world in 1987."

And we had hoped that there would be more editions of this. I certainly wasn't in a position to do that after a bit. This was sort of my big thing, and somebody else needed to run with it. I think the Netherlands did their own version of this maybe eight or nine years later. So, it did get replicated in some ways and used as a basis for other editions, but once the technology started getting so sophisticated, once we got the Internet and once we got full-text searching and all of the search capabilities that were possible, are possible, it's something that's much less needed.

People can pluck out of either Google or their own interest and find a language term in any piece of research published, or in a piece of media that's put out there. So, it's a much less needed thing, because this was clearly the era before full-text searching. I mean, back then, all of the documents, especially research and policy documents, anything was available only with the existing thesauri, and they shut out all the rest of us that didn't fit.

Belantara: You mentioned that you would share lists, you shared the categories, initially, when you came up with them and you would get feedback. So, you know, as you just mentioned, language is a living thing and people have different ideas, so how would you handle disagreements about terminology when you were creating the thesaurus?

Capek: Mostly with a sense of humor.

We didn't get into any knockdown, drag out fights about any of this; at least, that's my recollection. I did, to some extent, with Cheryl, my colleague in the Business and Professional Women's Foundation, because she wanted this as a very precise thesaurus, and I saw it much more as a living document. The example I tried to give her at the time was circumcision, and if you do a traditional breakdown of *Circumcision*, it's *Male circumcision* and *Female circumcision*, and male and female circumcision under circumcision, which is under surgical procedures, that completely and utterly distorts female circumcision, which is, essentially, violence against women, in my opinion.

So how do you do that? You have to break it apart. You have to be more creative. You have to be willing to say, "We're not going to do a traditional volume here. We're going to really bust things open. We're going to bust things open and make it work for how we have to make it work." And that's a lot of what we were trying to do. Or at least that's what my vision for it was. And I think most of the task force shared that.

Once we decided we were really out to bust up the traditional hierarchies—not just white male hierarchies, we were out there to bust up the traditional hierarchies in language—and how the traditional librarian documents the traditional thesauri would have forced us to arrange them, I mean, excuse my language, but it was essentially, "Fuck that!" There was no way I was going to put in all of my time and energy just to create and replicate the male hierarchy. And so that's really what the vision of this was. We were groundbreaking, and by golly, we were going to show it.

Belantara: Tell us about the work that was involved in creating all of the different displays. You have the alphabetical, the hierarchical, the rotated and delimiter displays. What kind of work was involved in creating each of those?

Capek: It wasn't much work. Those were traditional categories of a formal thesaurus, and they were tools—the structural tools that made the whole thing beautiful and made it work beautifully. And we got really lucky with our design team at Harper & Row because they were able to take these categories and use their design skills to make them much more usable, I think. And I mean, I didn't have a clue what those were initially.

Like I said earlier, *Roget* was my understanding of a thesaurus, but once we put all this together, coming at it with so many different angles of interaction was really fascinating. Seeing the language from different angles of vision was just really interesting to me.

Belantara: What role do you think race and class difference played in the creation of the thesaurus? How did you think about incorporating cultural differences in the selected terminology?

Capek: People were very tuned into that. A number of our centers had come up with ways of doing research bridging race, class, and gender, which is now standard jargon, but, back then, that was a whole new area to even think about. That got mentioned the very first meeting of the Council we ever had, and it was very much a priority, to look at all those different dimensions.

So, it was in everybody's mind, I think, when they were doing the work. And once we broke up into subject areas, it was much easier to take responsibility for that and make sure everybody had at least some sense of getting input from a broad range of, certainly, race; class, not so much, and, obviously, gender is key to the whole thing, but, you know, it was definitely on most people's minds.

Belantara: Many terms in the thesaurus are actually culturally specific. For example, in the thesaurus, there are the terms, and I could be pronouncing these incorrectly, but there's a listing for *Mikveh*, for example. How did the task force choose which cultural terms would be represented in the thesaurus?

Capek: Oh, that was really up to each subject group. It's what people shared with us from the subject groups. They really had the input on that. And what we tried to do was use the related terms, wherever possible, to link to those; so, that would give more definition. We obviously weren't writing a dictionary, so there aren't definitions there, but this is right about the time Cheris Kramarae and her colleagues were doing the *Feminist Dictionary*, which came out around the same time, and they were paired together as a really important resource. Some of the same terms would be in both of those, as tools for people to use.

Belantara: Tell us about any new terms that were introduced via the thesaurus. Could you tell us about any terms that were particularly meaningful to you personally, or to the communities you were working with?

Capek: There wasn't a lot that was new. The one I remember, that I hadn't known earlier, was *Contact dyke*. That was a joke for a lot of us, because what does that mean? Well, that means, you know, the lesbian in the community that you go to if you want to find out who else is doing what. So, somebody who knows, and there's usually at least one in every neighborhood. That kind of thing was—some of it was slang.

We tried not to, just as sort of as a general rule, include a lot of slang that would be quickly out of date. I mean, we were assuming this would last for maybe five years or so—that the thesaurus would quickly become outdated. I'm not sure how outdated it is.

The one group that I think, in retrospect, we didn't include enough of, was Native Americans. Because I'm very close friends with a Native American artist out here, and I gave her a copy of this, and I was aware as I was giving it to her that I was proud of it, and I wanted her to see what the work was, but that it was done in 1987, and a lot of us were then pretty clueless about Native American culture—still are, I mean, even here in New Mexico, it's amazing what little knowledge gets dispensed in the schools. And I've been doing other volunteer work to try to change some of that, but it's really, that's just one example where it's, you know, it's a flawed document.

We did the best we could with all the resources we had at the time and the money and the energy we had to do it. And you know, nobody is ever going to say, "This is the final, authoritative list." There is no such thing as an authoritative list! I see "authoritative list" and I want to say, "No, no authority!" But that's more me than what the thesaurus was. So, you know, I had to tone it down a little bit.

Belantara: Did Hana[9] have something to say there?

Crawford: I'm going to keep it running but I'm, you know, eavesdropping today, and I was wondering about sex work?

Capek: About?

Crawford: Sex work?

Capek: Yeah, it's there.[10] Yeah. Did you hear her?
Belantara: Yeah.

Capek: She said sex work.

Belantara: Yeah, sex work is in the thesaurus. Is that what you said, Mary Ellen?

Capek: Yeah, I think so. Let me look it up. We have *Sex tourism*, but sex work per se, no. *Sex tourism, Sex stereotypes, Sex selection, Segregation, Roles, Stereotyping, Reversal, Ratio, Pre-selection, Sex objects, Sex manuals, Sex industry, Sex hormones, Sex equity...*

Let's see what prostitution yields us. *Prostitution*, right across from *Provost*. "Prostitutes, link under related terms, *Camp followers, Concubinage, Courtesans, Geishas, Harlots, Johns, Pimps, Sex tourism, Sexual*

---

9. Hana Crawford is the sound recordist who was onsite with Capek during the recording of this interview.
10. Referring to the presence of the term "sex work" in the *Women's Thesaurus*.

exploitation, Sexually-transmitted disease. So, *Prostitution, Brothels— Economic value of women's work, Female sexual slavery, Massage parlors, Organized crimes, Sex tourism, Sexual exploitation, Sexually transmitted diseases, State regulations, Tricks, Violence against women...* So, you know, it's not complete, but we caught a lot of it.

Belantara: And so just a moment ago, you were saying there is no finalized list, right? But—

Capek: We would add *Sex work.*

Belantara: But at the same time, you had to finalize this iteration of this project. You mentioned before that there was something going on when you were coming up upon the final edits. So, once you did begin to finalize your word lists and decide on the structure, what was the next step? And what were you thinking during the final editing stage?

Capek: Well, it was absolutely an amazing experience, and it was pretty much the last year. I was doing the coordination still, but everybody was working well together at that point. It was mostly keeping everybody in the loop. But I was also trying to get a publisher, at the same time I was editing this thing, and we went through two publishers before we finally got to Harper & Row.

And that's a story that's worth telling, because we first went... I don't remember, I've suppressed the name of the first publisher. They were very interested, they wanted to do it. They were a library publisher, but they finally decided not to, because we were breaking down authority lists. We were a little too radical for their tastes.

Oxford University Press almost gave us a contract. In the final analysis, they decided, same thing, we were just a little too, you know, not normal. And somebody, I don't even remember who it was, got a blurb into this magazine, and an editor at Harper & Row named Janet Goldstein called me and she said, "Do you have a publisher yet for this document?"

And I said, "Nope, why, are you interested?"

And she said, "We are!"

And that's history. She was amazing. She totally got what we were trying to do. So did the designers; so did the editors. It was a cheering squad of people that we worked with at Harper & Row. They were absolutely wonderful, and that's what made the whole thing work. I don't remember where, in the sequence of things, that we got that contract. It was probably when I was partially through the final editing of it. We were going to go ahead and do the editing regardless, whether we had a publisher on hand, a traditional publisher, or not. I mean, we would've published it ourselves if we had to. Because we already, by then, had done a couple of reports that we self-published. But Harper & Row's design made the whole difference, for me at least, in the presentation of this and how it was so beautifully understood. It's accessible in a way that it otherwise wouldn't have been.

The other in-kind contribution we got—this was just total luck—we found a company called Advanced Data Management that was in a town called Kingston, which is right next to Princeton, and they were able to hook me up from Princeton, where I was living at the time, with a direct connection into their mainframe systems. They were the ones that designed the software to manage the whole thing, including all the displays. So, the editing that I got to do was using the screens they set up for me with each of the rotated displays, and it was just totally amazing that we had that connection and that opportunity. And that's pretty much all I did for six months.

I had long hair like yours at the time, and I would feel like I would put my head down and words would come tumbling out of my curly locks. It was so funny. And it was constant. I mean, it was total immersion because it was having to do both the hierarchies and the related terms. I mean, those were the two biggies: narrower term, broader terms, related terms. And using those tools to create the kinds of connections and pull apart the other things, like circumcision for example, that I was describing. And you know, let me just show you, give you an example of that. I'll look it up, female circumcision, instead of laying it out like that: *Female circumcision*, the subject group is *Natural sciences and health*, narrower terms are *Clitoridectomy* and *Vulvectomy*, related terms are *Castration, Chastity belts, Clitoris, Genital mutilation, Infibrillation, Initiation rites,* and *Tribal customs.*

So that was what we ended up with, pulling that apart. Otherwise, it would've probably still been in *Natural sciences and health.* Although, *Male circumcision* isn't really a... maybe that shouldn't be, technically, under sciences and health, because that's a religious practice most of the time. Let me just see here. It's under both *Natural sciences and health* and *Social sciences and culture. Surgical procedures, Penis and rites* are the related terms. So, there are two entirely different frameworks for that.

Belantara: So, you were doing all of this editing with the computer that the company set up for you?

Capek: I sat in my office at home in Princeton, and they had set up—I guess it must have been a modem, it would have to have been a modem, you know, the old kind that you put the phone in, or something like that. The old-fashioned modems, it would've been 1985 or 1986, so whatever modem was current back in '85 and '86, and I could dial into their mainframe. They were wonderfully supportive. They kept rolling their eyes, they thought the project was hilarious. The "Word Lady," as they called me. These are the hotshot tech guys that are used to much duller stuff, and we were the ladies talking about things like, you know, date rape and female clitoridectomies, right? So, it's a whole different world for these guys. They had never seen it before, but they were wonderfully helpful.

Belantara: So, you're sitting there, you're doing all of the final edits. At this point, were you already kind of committed to what you had decided would be the finished thesaurus? Or were you still, like, making some final changes at the end once you were there hooked up?

Capek: Oh, final changes all the way through it. Yeah, and it was easy to do. I mean, once we pretty much had the text, I don't remember the process. We may have done one of the displays, like the alphabetical display, and sent that to everybody on the committee and in the subject groups, and then gotten their feedback from it. Say, "Go through this with a fine-tooth comb. If there's anything you disagree with, let me know now, we could change it. It's not written in stone yet."

Even to the very end of this, we tried to keep an iterative process going.

Belantara: This is prior to actually publishing it, but how did you decide that it was ready for publication when it's a never-ending process? How did you finally say, "It's time"? How did you make that decision?

Capek: Well, it was obvious that we had to stop at some point because the money, certainly for my time, was not going to keep going. I had a lot of other things on my plate. I had to turn to the things I had put aside for this editing stuff. So, I had six months, I think that was what it was. And I did what I could in that time. And I had a sense we were pretty close to completion. You can tell that you're almost ready when there aren't a lot of suggestions for changes. And there was a point at which I think people said, "Okay, this is as good as this is going to get for now, write the introduction and let's just get it off our desks."

Belantara: When did the Library of Congress add the *Women's Thesaurus* to its official MARC Code List of thesauri, and were you consulted about this or asked before they added it?

Capek: I don't honestly remember. That's a question for Sarah Pritchard. She's the one who pulled that off. She's the one that was there at the Library of Congress. She was one of my main touchstones for suggestions and feedback, and I'm sure she took it and ran with it as far and as fast as she could go. I don't remember the timing of it. It probably was within a year or two that we had. Within the first year we got wonderful reviews. It won awards. Everybody was knocked over. "This was such an important project." "We loved what you did." "Yada, yada, yada yada."

It hit the stands and really made a good impression. So wherever possible, people were trying to take it seriously. It helped that Harper & Row published it; it helped that we had Harvard, Wellesley, Stanford, Rutgers, University of Tennessee, and the University of Texas. We had all of the major universities on our plate working with us. So, I mean, we were an impressive-looking group, and people had to take us seriously, and they did.

UNIVERSITY OF CALIFORNIA, BERKELEY

BERKELEY · DAVIS · IRVINE · LOS ANGELES · RIVERSIDE · SAN DIEGO · SAN FRANCISCO   SANTA BARBARA · SANTA CRUZ

WOMEN'S RESOURCE CENTER LIBRARY
(415) 643-8367

100 T-9 BUILDING
BERKELEY, CALIFORNIA 94720

July 27, 1989

Sally H. McCallum
Network Development and
  MARC Standards Office
LM 327
Library of Congress
Washington, D.C. 20540

Dear Ms. McCallum:

I am writing to request that A Women's Thesaurus by the National Council for Research on Women be added to the MARC list of thesauri used by your office.

I have been using this thesaurus to catalog our collection, and will need your "blessing" in order to eventually have my records added to the Main Library's catalog database.

If I am not being clear, or if there is a problem with what I am asking would you call me? Otherwise, I look forward to hearing that you have added the Women's Thesaurus to your official list.

Sincerely,

Nancy Humphreys

Nancy Humphreys
Librarian

cc. National Council for Research on Women (Mary Ellen Capek)

Figure 5. A letter to Sally McCallum from Nancy Humphreys to suggest the *Women's Thesaurus* be added to the MARC list of thesauri.

THE LIBRARY OF CONGRESS
WASHINGTON, D.C. 20540

SEP 14 1989

NETWORK DEVELOPMENT AND
MARC STANDARDS OFFICE

September 6, 1989

Dear Ms. Humphreys:

Based on your request of July 27, 1989, we have assigned the code "wot" to the publication A Women's Thesaurus (New York: Harper & Row). The code is to be used in subfield ‡2 (Source of heading or term) of 6XX subject heading fields.

Code "wot" will be published in Part IV (Subject/Index Term Sources) of the USMARC Code List for Relators, Sources, Description Conventions when the publication is reissued.

Sincerely,

Sally H. McCallum
Chief, Network Development and
MARC Standards Office

cc: National Council for Research on Women (Mary-Ellen Capek)
Phyllis Bruns, Net Dev/MSO

Ms. Nancy Humphreys
Women's Resource Center Library
100 T-9 Building
University of California, Berkeley
Berkeley, CA 94720

Figure 6. A letter from Sally McCallum to Nancy Humphreys indicating that the Library of Congress' MARC Standards Office assigned a USMARC code to the *Women's Thesaurus.*

Belantara: How do you feel that it was added to the official list?

Capek: Wonderful. That's something I brag on all the time, that, in retrospect, you know, it's interesting because you get to be eighty years old, which I turned in December, one of the things you do is look back and think, "Okay, what's this all been about? What have I understood? What have I done? What do I still need to do?" All of that. A very retrospective thinking. And in retrospect, the thesaurus is really the centerpiece of what I've done. It's the thing I'm proudest of. I think it's the thing, in the long run, that's probably made the most difference, and it's just something I really am grateful for having had the opportunity to do. I mean, I always struggle between wanting to be more of a poet, a writer, and I do a lot of that, but my basic instinct is toward change—trying to make change happen, however I can, wherever I can.

And that thesaurus was one of those documents that kind of combined both of those areas that mean so much to me. And I mean, how good is that? It was just amazing to have had that opportunity. And you know, the Council used that. It gave the Council credibility. That was also another piece of the puzzle for us as we were starting to create this coalition. We needed something that would kick it off, that says, "Wow, we do know what we're doing." And that really helped because the reviews were so good. We got a lot of positive feedback from a lot of different places, which helped us get better funding as we moved along.

Belantara: You've mentioned that you had really positive reviews. In addition to that, do you know if the *Women's Thesaurus* was put into use by different libraries or other organizations?

Capek: Yeah, it was used in a lot of different places. I can't recall—I don't have lists of those, but I do know from a lot of people that it was used for, you know, predominantly cataloging, for cleaning up, once we got it into the Library of Congress, in the MARC system, you know, a lot of that just happened. So, it wasn't even needing to be a choice on people's part. Women's studies programs, I didn't get a hold of Hilda's example until just recently. And I just absolutely love it, because I used to do the same thing even after it was edited. After all that editing I did, you know, ten years after the fact, I'd sit down and open up a page and read it.

We even had a dramatic reading of the section, "Images of Women" at one of our board meetings. It was absolutely hilarious. We'd all had a little bit of wine by then. But our then board chair, Catherine Stimson, who was just hilarious, very dramatic, she went on to become one of the MacArthur Foundation's people within the foundation that awarded the Genius Grants and she ended up just doing this dramatic reading of

"Images of Women," and we were all hysterical by the end of it; it was so funny.

So, you could just go in, open it and you know, open a page and you know, get inspired or laugh. A mental health break is really what we were trying for there. You know, in retrospect, that's one of the things I'm trying to write about now. You don't, as women, even in our era now, we still live in a world where we don't see ourselves reflected, even if we're white, upper middle-class women with a lot of privilege. We don't see ourselves reflected back very often, and it goes on and on and on. And one of the things Hilda said was that it felt like, to her, it connected her to a community of like-minded women that she felt were working on the same concerns and same language and same issues.

Belantara: And so just one quick follow-up question: what happened to the task force's documentation after the thesaurus was published?

Capek: It's all in the archives up at Schlesinger. We started getting all of that in order, and being taught how to archive, which was not necessarily instinctive, right? You just send the folders, you don't mess with them, you don't clean them out ahead of time. We started archiving, probably late '80s, early '90s with that, especially because we had to move our office in early '90. And so, a lot of the files from the early years were just sent up to Harvard, to Radcliffe's Schlesinger Library, which is a wonderful, wonderful resource.

Belantara: And so, is this housed under a wider collection under the Council?

Capek: Yeah, it would be with the Council's archives.

Belantara: And there's somewhere in there, the *Women's Thesaurus* folder, or—

Capek: Yeah.

Belantara: Box?

Capek: Yes, it's all there. Boxes and boxes of it, I expect. I'm sure the early lists are all there too, so if some poor graduate student decides they want a project to go back and decide how lists evolved, that's one way to do it. I mean, it's a very interesting linguistic exercise, actually, but you know, what we were concentrating on at the time was being very pragmatic about it.

Belantara: What do you think of the *Women's Thesaurus* now? And would you change anything? Do you have any advice for anyone taking on an alternative thesaurus or classification project now?

Capek: One of the things I was very proud of, and I think worked very well, was the iterative process, and casting a net as broadly as possible, with people who have different access to the language and just bringing in as many different voices as possible, because they spark each other. That's one of the things I saw happen over and over again in the Council that I'm very proud of actually.

I try, on a panel, to get a researcher, a policy person and an activist, and they would get really grumpy at first because nobody was speaking the same language or they weren't using the same words. They would have different meetings in different contexts. So, they would have to leave aside the usual frameworks and engage differently. And that really helped to get much more interesting thinking together happening. And I think that's what happens when you do a process like this—you have different voices, different perspectives, and it just really sparks everybody.

It's really important to be able to include as many different voices as possible in a project like this. But you've got to have also, at the same time, somebody that's willing to wrangle it and keep it in control. So, it's an interesting process. I wouldn't want to do it again, but I'm very glad I got to do it.

Belantara: I wanted to leave a little bit of space for you, Mary Ellen, if I missed anything that I should have asked you about, or if you just have any thoughts that you would like to share before we close out?

Capek: I just think that it's such an important way of framing stuff, and I'm so grateful you're doing this Ways of Knowing project because it's so important to make that much more public. People don't really get that there are different ways of knowing, and the more we learn how to understand other people's frameworks, the kinder we are, the more we learn how to engage with them differently, but also because there are so many groups that have been excluded by the use of language.

I mean, that's really what I'm trying to write about now, that so many people have used language as a bludgeon to really get rid of so many others that they don't fit in the mainstream. It's not easy because, a lot of times, you name stuff and people go, "Uh-oh, we weren't supposed to talk about that. That's a taboo."

But you know if it makes people nervous, that's exactly what you're supposed to talk about, especially if it's within an organization. So that's what I'm playing around with now. But the bottom line with all of this is that I'm very proud of this project and I really am hugely grateful that I got to do it.

Sarah M. Pritchard on the Women's Thesaurus

Biography

Sarah M. Pritchard retired in 2023 after sixteen years as the Dean of Libraries and the Charles Deering McCormick University Librarian at Northwestern University. She administered five libraries and the NU Press. She was previously University Librarian at the University of California, Santa Barbara; Director of Libraries at Smith College; associate executive director at the Association of Research Libraries; and reference specialist in women's studies at the Library of Congress.

She was on boards in the Big Ten Academic Alliance, the Association of Research Libraries, and the Center for Research Libraries, on the council of the American Library Association, and one of the founders of the ALA-ACRL Women's and Gender Studies Section. She has published over seventy articles, was the editor of *portal: Libraries and the Academy* for six years, and has lectured widely on library management, women's studies, digital systems, and other professional issues.

Pritchard received a BA from the University of Maryland and master's degrees in French and in Library Science from the University of Wisconsin-Madison. She received the ALA Equality Award, the ACRL Career Achievement Award in Women's Studies, the distinguished alumna award from the University of Wisconsin School of Library and Information Studies, and several awards for her work at the Library of Congress.

About the Interview

The following transcribed interview of Sarah M. Pritchard took place on June 22, 2022, as part of the *Ways of Knowing Oral History Project*. The interview was auto transcribed and then edited by Amanda Belantara and Emily Drabinski. Care was taken to not alter the original transcription's contents. However, the editors have formatted the following to improve readability and provided footnotes for clarity where appropriate. The original transcript and recording can be accessed through the *Ways of Knowing Oral History Project* held at NYU Libraries.[1]

Transcript from the *Ways of Knowing Oral History Project*

Interviewee: Sarah M. Pritchard, retired Dean of Libraries and Charles Dearing McCormick University Librarian at Northwestern University and member, The Women's Thesaurus Task Force
Interviewers: Emily Drabinski & Amanda Belantara
Date: June 22, 2022
Location: Virtual Interview; Evanston, Illinois

Amanda Belantara: Today we're interviewing Sarah M. Pritchard, Dean of Libraries and Charles Dearing McCormick University Librarian

---

1. Pritchard's recording is available here: https://search.library.nyu.edu/permalink/01NYU_INST/1d6v258/alma990098389930107871.

at Northwestern University. The interview was conducted for the *Ways of Knowing Oral History Project*. The interview took place virtually on June 22nd, 2022, and was recorded locally by Steven A. Poon at Northwestern University Library. The interviewers are Amanda Belantara and Emily Drabinski.

Belantara: Hi Sarah. We're interested in hearing a little bit about your background in education. Can you tell us how you became a librarian?

Sarah M. Pritchard: I became a librarian after I was already in graduate school studying French and Italian literature and did not find that career path very compelling to me. And libraries were something I had always thought I might want to work in. I wasn't sure, but I happened to be at a university that had a very good library school. So, I was already in one graduate program and applied to enroll the following year in the library science program. And right away I was extremely engaged by what I was learning within a week or two of starting courses in not just library science, but the role of libraries in society. And I just found it compelling. And so it was a continuous move for me from education in the humanities and languages and literatures into academically oriented library sciences.

I pretty much always was intending to work in colleges or universities or perhaps large municipal libraries that are like New York Public or Boston Public. I was looking at that time for large collections-centric libraries. But over my career I actually became quite fascinated by areas of services and technologies. So not literally just collections, but it was a steady gradual progression. It was also during my time in library science in graduate school in the mid-1970s that Madison, Wisconsin, was a hotbed of progressive activism. And it was while I was there that I started learning an enormous amount about the field of women's studies, which was in its infancy and, more importantly perhaps, the activism around equity issues for women, librarians, and women as customers in public libraries. So there was a convergence that started right at the beginning of my career between the academic fields of women's studies and the professional equity issues of women in the library profession.

Emily Drabinski: When you were getting your library degree in Madison, it sounds like that was a time of social change and social upheaval. Can you say something about what that was like, particularly in Madison, at the time?

Pritchard: It was a terribly exciting time to be in Madison, and I had been an undergraduate at the University of Maryland, which had a certain amount of activism, but we were always envious of other campuses. When we were at the University of Maryland, we always wished we were at Berkeley or Ann Arbor. And it was like, why doesn't our campus have lots of cool activism? I mean, we had some, you know, I was tear-gassed in an anti-war demonstration at Maryland.[2] We weren't lacking in activism, but it wasn't as cool a community.

So when I first came to the University of Wisconsin, boy was it cool. I was so excited to be living in Madison. The actual downtown area of Madison was full of stores that catered to activists. We had the Maoist bookstore and the feminist bookstore, and the university was coming off an earlier heyday of activism in the late sixties and early seventies that still lingered. I was there from 1975 to 1977, and there was still a huge, almost embedded fabric of activism; there were food co-ops, there were political co-ops, not just student activism, but the local community people.

The political scene too—who ran for mayor while I was a student there was a former student activist, one of the group who had gone underground and were wanted for bombing activities, who was rearrested finally. So, there was a trial, there was a resurgence in activism because of that. It was a heady time in Madison coming off a number of years of such activism, and I loved it, I loved it, I was just very ready for being very engaged and participatory; and, in the library science program, it translated into a lot of almost shoe leather.

We were ourselves organizing, we were demonstrating, we were going to community centers. We were talking about information for the peo-

---

2. Pritchard attended the University of Maryland from 1971 to 1975. During this time, U.S. universities saw significant student protests in response to the ongoing war in Vietnam.

ple and what was the role of librarians in community activism. So it was all of a piece; I really didn't want to leave but, of course, I needed a job. Many people who I went to school with at that time never did leave, even though they couldn't immediately get a professional job; they just wanted to stay in that area. And this is true—I've seen it with people in Berkeley and Ann Arbor—these communities have a magnetism that draws people.

Drabinski: You began working in libraries. You graduated and you began working in the Library of Congress in the 1980s, is that right?

Pritchard: 1977.

Drabinski: Can you tell us a little bit about the working and professional environment for a reference librarian working at the Library of Congress?

Pritchard: When I first came to the Library of Congress, I came on what was then a very well-known internship program; the Library of Congress had it for many years, they would recruit both internally and externally and they would put together a cohort every year that spent five or six months moving through the whole library undertaking projects and being given workshops and lectures about every aspect of library operations. And so, it was basically a group of twelve people: six new library science graduates and six existing workers, junior level librarians from internally.

This was a wonderful way to start work at such a large place; at the time I was there, Library of Congress had 5,000 employees. I think it's down to about 3,000 now. But it was an intimidatingly large place. And, of course, just being the Library of Congress as an entity was intimidating. So, the intern program was a fantastic introduction to cataloging, acquisitions, copyright, congressional research, reference, and every aspect. And we had an opportunity to really learn about different areas where we might eventually want to work.

We were not necessarily guaranteed a specific slot at the end of that program, however; the idea was to keep on the lookout for openings because, of course, in a place that large, there were always openings, there was always a lot of turnover. I very much wanted a job in public services, and I was quite lucky to actually get one. But it was not immediately like, "Oh yes, Sarah, we're going to give you a reference job."

So, I competed successfully for an entry level reference job at a time when they were expanding reference services to have more reference librarians at different service points. They were introducing more user-centric services, and right in my first year or two there was sort of a reader's advisory desk right at the front of the reading room—which was a new service to try to help orient researchers—as well as the central reference area. And there was also a brand-new online catalog when that kind of thing was really unheard of. And we had a reference librarian helping people use this old VT100 terminal interface, a very command-line type of online catalog.

Most people had no idea even how to look up a subject heading; we didn't have free text searching. It was in the pre-Google era. In my early days at the Library of Congress, it was, even though it was sort of all about reference, there was a great diversity. We also had a telephone reference for any kind of outside callers; there was a little nook inside that huge main reading room where there was telephone reference. There was a reference librarian where you turned in your stack requests because when you got your request back saying, "Sorry, that book's not available," you often needed help.

So, right away, I was working in an environment of user-oriented multiple types of reference services, and there was a big increase in user instruction and in preparation of printed materials to go along with that. It was very fruitful, and I learned a lot about online catalogs and how to deal with people who are doing research in a closed stack environment. Every once in a while, we could give somebody a stack pass, but we had to interview them about their research and make sure, have you really exhausted the tertiary bibliographies that could help you decide what books you need to request? Yes or no.

In the job series that I was part of, there was a built-in promotion progression for those public services librarians where, in order to progress through the three-step civil service grade progression, you had to develop a subject specialty. So, once I'd been there about a year or two as I was going through a performance evaluation, I was asked, "And what do you intend to target to develop over the next year or two into a subject specialty?"

And the first couple of things I proposed were areas that were already being covered by other specialists. I was told, "Well, you know, somebody already does that."

At the time I had no academic training in women's studies, but I was an activist in the field and I knew people and I said, "Well, I would love to do women's studies. I don't have any academic classwork, I don't have any professional credentials, but I'm really super interested in this emerging field."

And to my surprise and pleasure, they said, "Oh great, we need that, we're getting lots of questions, we're getting lots of books. We don't have someone who's the official specialist. People are doing it sort of casually, but you know, you go girl."

So, I became the women's studies specialist at a time of incredible flowering of that field and also a time when librarians were coming together with both activists and faculty to try to develop resources like anthologies, bibliographies, guidebooks. How do you do research in this field where the subject headings are terrible and maybe there are just not enough books?

Drabinski: Can you tell us some of the challenges you faced when trying to provide reference service for questions related to women?

Pritchard: Well, terrible subject headings—we were in a card catalog era, so it was a very structured card cataloging environment compared to today's metadata, and without free text searching of what we call pre-coordinated subject headings, we had to do a lot of work with scholars and users to try to translate their research questions into the best subject headings. And many books had very vague or broad subject headings. You'd go to the card catalog and there'd be a hundred cards under some really useless broad subject heading, and it was a lot of headings, like, *Women* *in—, Women as—*; there was a lot of extra insight that you had to bring to helping researchers. There were very few bibliographies specifically on women's studies or women's history.

You had to learn a lot about what terms were used by other subject bibliographies in order to get into the material. So really the access was hampered by poor cataloging, vague cataloging, sexist terminology. And then the resources—you often had to be very creative about primary sources. There were really great primary sources if you could finally find them. But often there was a lot of training with faculty to use a primary source that they didn't realize would help them because it wouldn't be like a book that said how to track women's lives, but you could go by your own knowledge of the collections. You could show a researcher how to use Sanborn maps to show how women lived in a certain town.[3] But those Sanborn maps sure weren't in the catalog that way.

Things like property ownership and wills and business records all were under husbands' names because women weren't allowed to own property. Working with people to try to show them how to decipher these sources when you just didn't have the metadata, the cataloging, even the indexing was very challenging. And then, gradually, more and more new sources started arriving on the scene. And one of the good things at the Library of Congress is we were so comprehensive in our acquisitions. Even if these sources came from ephemeral or fringy places, we would go ahead and collect them, whereas, in many university libraries, if it wasn't emerging from a major publisher, they weren't going to buy it. But we had stuff coming in through copyright deposit.

I was able to actually retain a lot of materials and put those into bibliographies that would then help other librarians; librarians working together to make sure that somebody was acquiring things somewhere. Also, it motivated a lot of us in the American Library Association who were working with researchers, as to how can we make sure the resources get created, and work with publishers to get more book reviews so that

---

3. The Sanborn Map Company produced detailed maps of urban environments that were used by the fire insurance industry in the late 19th century. They continue to be used as primary sources for historians interested in a range of research questions about how Americans lived during this period.

other libraries would buy it. We worked with a lot of indexing companies to try to get more women's periodicals indexed in things like *Reader's Guide*[4]; there was only one index that really covered women's periodicals. When the *Women's Review of Books*[5] first came out, it wasn't being covered. We got mobilized to get periodicals included in indexes.

Drabinski: Were you involved in the 1982 ad hoc ALA Task Force on Women's Studies Database Evaluation?

Pritchard: I sure was, and I published a great article based on that project.[6]

So much of the recent activism over especially racist subject headings, just makes me both happy and sad thinking that, well, we were working on this stuff forty years ago trying to get things changed. It just takes a very long time...

Drabinski: Can you briefly describe your work with that task force?

Pritchard: We were concerned that there weren't any databases just in women's studies. So people were resorting to figuring out: How do you use *Psych Abstracts* or the *MLA Index*? What vocabularies are used? What periodicals are covered in those indexes?

So, we decided different librarians would focus on different indexes and we would write up our assessment of whether that index was any good to use for women's studies. We had to develop some evaluation cri-

---

4. The *Reader's Guide to Periodical Literature*.
5. The *Women's Review of Books* was a feminist journal intended to promote women's creative writing and scholarship and to connect this work to feminist activism. Linda Gardiner was the founding editor of the *Women's Review*, which began publishing in 1983.
6. Pritchard, Sarah M., "Developing Criteria for Database Evaluation: The Example of Women's Studies," *Reference Librarian* 4, np. 11 (1984): 247-261, DOI: 10.1300/j120v04n11_19.

teria. And that was the particular part that I worked on because I had already been active in what we used to call the Machine Assisted Reference Section (MARS, part of ALA), on how to evaluate databases because databases were brand new then.

Users didn't do their own searching, librarians did the searching. It was very expensive and you wanted to evaluate search processes. So, I was already somewhat active in how to evaluate database searching. I took that knowledge and worked on specific criteria for evaluating coverage and quality in women's studies: what magazines were being covered; what indexing languages were being used. We developed a set of criteria and we carried out a bunch of evaluations. And then I wrote it up into a nice little article and got that published.

Drabinski: In your chapter, "Developing Criteria for Database Evaluation: The Example of Women's Studies," you wrote: "The increased awareness of sexism and other biases in language has led to the use of many new terms and phrases. If these are not found in database thesauri, the very point of the research may be obscured, and the evaluation criteria includes a section on vocabulary and indexing."[7]

Can you tell us what the committee found when they were evaluating databases at the time? And, do you think that much has changed since then?

Pritchard: Well, it was a real patchwork. There was no consistency in terminology because each database came from a different publisher, and these were mostly abstracting and indexing databases that indexed the journal literature, not as much monographic literature. So, they all had their own internal indexing languages that they used for old-style printed indexes, which were then converted into online indexes. So, you had

---

7. Pritchard, S. M., "Developing Criteria for Database Evaluation: The Example of Women's Studies," in *Evaluation of Reference Services*, ed. Linda S. Katz (New York: Routledge, 1985): 274-261.

MEDLINE[8], you had *Social Sciences Citation Index*[9], you had *Psych Abstracts*[10], you had all these indexes, many of which had just converted from a printed form and had not really expanded to a multiplicity of headings.

They would assign two or three indexing terms to an article, and we had to look at the actual thesaurus used by each publisher. What is the indexing language used in *Social Science Citation Index*, for example? And do they also index the author's abstract if the author supplies one? Do they pick up on those terms in addition to the tags that they add themselves?

We found a lot of unevenness and inconsistency and lack of the contemporary terminology that was very rapidly emerging in the women's studies field. Everybody was coming up with new terminology for the concepts themselves that were new in feminist discourse. Some of this was coming from activists and some of this was coming from historians, you know? I remember the first time I heard the term *looksism*,[11] it was like, well, what's that? And that was new. And that, of course, was not in the indexing languages, but that was starting to be a term used in feminist activist magazines.

Obviously, this leads to the *Women's Thesaurus*, as you can imagine. In addition to everything we found for the indexing languages, we also had the problem of the Library of Congress Subject Headings for the monographic literature, which we weren't even looking at in that particular article. I think things have evolved rapidly in the indexing languages for the journal literature, partly because the journal articles themselves are using these terms. So, it's in people's abstracts, but also, frankly, in the advent of free text searching.

---

8. *MEDLINE* is the bibliographic database of the National Library of Medicine indexed using Medical Subject Headings (MeSH).

9. The *Social Sciences Citation Index* is a multidisciplinary index of social sciences literature. It was originally developed by the Institute for Scientific Information and is now distributed by Clarivate.

10. *Psychological Abstracts* is a database of scholarly journals in psychology produced by the American Psychological Association.

11. A term referring to discrimination against people considered to be unattractive; now more frequently referred to as lookism.

It's a little more difficult to do free text searching because you have to sort of guess after the fact. But on the other hand, you have a lot more terminology that you can try. And most databases, now you just have far greater penetration of the article itself, depth of text that can be searched. So, what the specific terminology is that's being used by a certain publisher is a little less crucial. But it has improved. And again, partly because publishers and databases are looking at the most current literature, they're looking at that year's journal literature. And we found that terminology changes much more rapidly in the journal literature and publishers will respond to that. In the monographic literature, it changes more slowly because it's based in turn on the journal literature.

Changes in history or sociology monographs aren't going to show up in an actual book for a couple years after they've already been in wide use in the journal literature, and the Library of Congress Subject Headings were very conservative. They were very reluctant to introduce new headings until they saw it, not just once, but in enough monographic literature that they could say this is really emerging. So that meant by default you weren't going to see changes in subject headings for sometimes as long as four or five years after you had already seen that in the journal literature. It was a trailing impact trailing through the monographic literature and there was a lot of concern about that. And even working within the Library of Congress itself as a reference librarian, I did not have authority to demand changes in the subject headings. We could send suggestions, but there was a very intense review and vetting process for changes in the subject headings that was very slow.

It still is as we see even now, after forty years. And we still see the difficulty recently with getting the heading for *Illegal aliens* finally changed. So much of the recent activism over especially racist subject headings just makes me both happy and sad thinking that, well, we were working on this stuff forty years ago trying to get things changed. It just takes a very long time, and some pressure works better than others. Some people have more sway than others in bringing these changes about, and, often, grassroots activists are not the ones that the Library of Congress is listening to or some major publisher that is producing a large database.

Belantara: Can you tell us about the *Women's Thesaurus* and its goals?

Pritchard: The *Women's Thesaurus* was a project of the National Council for Research on Women, which had just come into being a few years earlier, that had emerged from a lot of academic women's centers. The National Women's Studies Association was brand new, but they were really a focus on individual scholars and students. The National Council for Research on Women, which benefited from a lot of foundation funding early on, was really looking to coordinate the research centers that were starting to grow on campuses. A great many colleges and universities, and sometimes independent organizations, were setting up basically research centers in the same era as the UN Decade for Women. It is not to be underestimated, the impact of the UN Decade for Women on the founding of these centers for research.

Because of the demand, we needed more bona fide research about the status of women in this country or that country, or we needed more historical research. So, the National Council for Research on Women was rapidly building coordination across the centers that were members of the council, and they started, of course, publishing directories of all the centers: Where are all the women's centers? Who publishes what? Which women's centers publish a newsletter? And quickly from that emerged: Which women's centers are collecting what? Who's got a library focused on that topic at that women's center? And at these women's centers, you often had a lot of specialized ephemeral literature. If you were the research center in one particular area, you might have had a lot of pamphlet material, for example, from one area of work; like, say it was abortion rights or women's development work in Africa.

The council became very interested in trying to not only connect the centers but connect the resources that were being collected and published by the centers in order to develop a database that would include all the centers. The thesaurus then evolved because we realized we needed a consistent indexing language, and we couldn't use the indexing languages of other publishers because it was not adequate. But really, the thesaurus evolved out of a desire to connect the centers that were members of the council and the resources that the centers were developing, either through publications or collections. Then, how do we help these centers catalog these mini branch libraries, all these scattered little collections in these different centers?

People were starting to use homegrown database software. People were growing a little file on their brand-new little Macintosh computer in their office, but they were using very inconsistent practices across the different centers. Our desire was if everybody could use the same thesaurus, it would be far easier to connect all these fantastic but disparate little collections in the women's centers around the country. And that was both research centers at universities and activist centers or places like the American Association of University Women, which had a huge headquarters library, or the Business and Professional Women's Foundation, which was almost a hundred-year-old organization with a big library aimed at professional women. There was a convergence through the Council of new centers focused on women's studies research and universities and some of these more longstanding centers aimed at women in the professions and women's international development. That's what was getting a huge benefit from the UN Decade as well. So, the thesaurus was a desire to connect women's centers and the resources they were developing.

Belantara: And how did you become involved with the thesaurus project?

Pritchard: Well, I was already involved with the center.[12] I remember the first time I met Mary Ellen Capek at a meeting in New York City, and I don't remember whether she had called that meeting, and there were two or three librarians, and the Feminist Task Force was already known, and because we published things, and so it may have been that, you know, some friend of a friend, somehow a connection was made by people working at the Council. Maybe one of the member centers had a librarian on their campus who had said, you know, how do we find out more about this council?

---

12. The women's centers organized under the National Council for Research on Women.

It's sort of lost to my memory how that first connection was made. Mary Ellen might remember, or somebody like Sue Searing might remember—Sue's *Bibliography*, which was actually started by Esther Stineman.[13] The Esther Stineman bibliography was a watershed in women's studies reference books that came out from the University of Wisconsin, and it may have been by seeing that bibliography that people at the Council said, "Hey, you know, we need to get in touch with some of these librarians."

There was a small number of librarians who were invited to a meeting at the National Council for Research on Women. And it may have been because people at the Council became aware of some of the early bibliography work that librarians were doing; the Council was an organization of centers. If you were a women's center at a university or an independent organization, you could join the National Council for Research on Women. Centers were motivated to do that because of the connections that they could then make with each other. The National Council was seeking grants to fund projects and was seeking to connect women's centers because those were its main members. You could also affiliate as an individual, but the primary membership of the Council was other centers, academic research centers in women's studies and women's history.

Belantara: Which center were you affiliated with at the time?

Pritchard: None. So, the librarians were kind of a side group that was developed by direct relationships with the folks at the council, and we started this work with them. Then, several of us joined as individual affiliates, but we became a project of the council. Now some of us worked on campuses where there was a center, but at the time I was at the Library of Congress, there was not a center. In Washington DC there were several organizations that were centers, but my work with the Council really came about because the Council convened a librarian's group.

---

13. Loeb, C., Searing, S., and Stineman E., *Women's Studies: A Recommended Core Bibliography, 1980-1985* (Littleton, CO: Libraries Unlimited, 1987).

Belantara: Thank you for clarifying. And so, what was your role in the task force and how was labor divided?

Pritchard: Well, I don't frankly remember how labor was divided, but we started collectively in the task force developing word lists, and different people took on different subject areas, and Mary Ellen was coordinating all of it. And I went back looking in my folder and I have all these typescripts and mimeographs of these word lists. We kept trying to think of all possible language. We were trying not to duplicate existing indexing languages, or thesauri; we didn't want to just recreate the Library of Congress Subject Headings, we wanted to really focus on the distinctive language, the distinctive terminology. And we looked a lot at: What were the collections in the different centers? What language was needed? What were those broad subject areas?

So, we started developing word lists and then the librarians really came to our area of excellence, if you will, in exploring syndetic structure. Syndetic structure is the web created by cross references. When you have a thesaurus, you have to look at which is a broader term, which is a narrower term, and which is a parallel term. And you set up all these references like *see* and *see also*, broader and narrower. That's what makes a thesaurus sort of magic is the syndetic structure. And that's what we were able to start shaping with this committee: we've got to bring a structure to this thesaurus, it can't be just an A-to-Z list, it's got to have cross referencing, it's got to have *see also* and *see* references and that kind of structure; and, of course, it is very intellectual, almost argumentative work. Is this broader, is this narrower, is this the better term? Which one do we want to use?

This went on for quite some time and I had sort of lost awareness of that until I went back looking at all these copies of word lists. Mary Ellen Capek rode herd on all of it, so she set the deadlines early on. I was so impressed with her level of ambition. She had decided this was going to be a published work. She was the one talking to publishers and really corralling all the content, and we were providing the professional expertise on what is a thesaurus, how it needed to function, and also constantly refining or expanding or both of the actual terminology. I don't remember that I individually had a special role. It was very collective work.

Belantara: Could you talk next about how the task force went about securing funding for this project?

Pritchard: I was not involved with that at all. That would be Mary Ellen's area. She was prodigious at reaching out and she had access to very supportive women funders at the Ford Foundation. Mariam Chamberlain of the Ford Foundation was another very powerful figure in the early years of the Council and women's centers. Mary Ellen did most of the work on securing grants and funding and endorsements from people at foundations. And she also did most of the work interviewing publishers based on insight from the librarians as to how to make sure this book had credibility and was properly published and not just a sort of a little quicky vanity press.

We wanted this thesaurus to have as much credibility as possible. We wanted it to be seen as a valid supplement in libraries that were already using the LC Subject Headings or the Sears List in a Dewey library. We wanted this to be seen as an acceptable augmentation. We were very aware of the rigidity that many cataloging departments had about what terminology they were allowed to use. We wanted to do everything we could to ensure that this thesaurus would have credibility in that world. I didn't personally work on any of the grants.

Belantara: And so, the goal then was never to develop an entirely new system—the idea was to really augment the existing systems.

Pritchard: That was my perception. I don't know if everybody felt that. If you were a standalone women's center, you might only have needed this thesaurus but if you were a university library, it would be more of an augmentation. I think we hoped it would be both. If you were a specialized center or small library and this was your only subject area, maybe this would fill all your needs. But in a larger library with so many other fields, they weren't going to stop using the other standardized indexing language and subject heading work.

Belantara: And so, you already talked about this just a little bit, but I was wondering if you could tell us a bit more about how the work actually got started.

Pritchard: It was always only ever eight or ten people. So, it wasn't a mass outreach to all the centers except through the Council itself. Because the centers were members of the council. The task force was mostly librarians and Mary Ellen Capek and maybe somebody else from the Council. And frankly, I don't remember the day to day how we worked on it. There was a lot of exchanging of photocopies of lists. We had email, but barely, and we didn't have online documents sharing. People didn't yet use email attachments even. So, it was still a lot of paper-based work.

We would meet as a committee during ALA, or during the early years at conferences of the National Women's Studies Association. As I said, more of the logistics were all being managed by Mary Ellen Capek. As I look back on it, I don't know how she did it, frankly. She was just like the Energizer Bunny or something. I don't mean to be patronizing, but she was just tireless in her ambition to see this project to fruition. And the vision was connecting the centers and she really had this great vision for how to get this huge body of information that was quite different from traditional library collections, you know—how to span this huge body of an emerging field and very interdisciplinary international grassroots information as well as more vetted research information—how to bring that all together.

Belantara: And so, you've got this stack of photocopied lists. What was the next step then? Let's say you receive a stack in the mail or at an in-person meeting at ALA—what happened next?

Pritchard: Kind of a brain gap for me. Mary Ellen started, or she must have had a project assistant working with her at the Council, started inputting all of this information to consolidate draft texts, and at some point, eventually, there were even galleys, but I don't remember being as deeply involved at that stage. I certainly remember vetting various specific areas of terminology and parts of the list, but I wasn't involved in the actual assembly of the document.

Belantara: We understand that terms from thirty-five research centers, libraries, publishers, and associations were used. How were these identified and selected? And how did they provide their list to the task force? Did any of these organizations' terms stand out or have a predominant impact on the task forces work?

Pritchard: So, I can't answer that last piece at all as to which had the most distinctive or influential lists. But I do remember Mary Ellen, and, again, because these were the member centers of the National Council, the council reached out and got lists from everybody they could. And we looked at all those lists. I do remember going through all of those. And, of course, there was some overlap and some complete areas of non-overlap, and we sought to consolidate those terms. We did a huge aggregation and then a weeding-out process. But different librarians might have specifically been fascinated by the list from this or that or the other research center; I don't remember myself. I mean, some of the centers had much bigger libraries, so by definition, you know, there was more terminology coming from them because they just had a larger task that they had already undertaken.

Belantara: In working on this project, were there any learning curves for you or for the group?

Pritchard: Compiling a thesaurus from scratch is really very complex. And it was actually a subject I thought I was familiar with because, even when I was still in graduate school, I had written a paper about how to develop multilingual thesauri. What did you do if you were a publisher with a database that had to reach out to multiple countries? This was a very interesting concern at the time. And because of my background in languages, I really thought this would be a great term paper topic, which turned out to be far more complicated. I had really bitten off more than I could chew as a grad student, but my faculty at the time were very supportive.

It's like, "Oh, Sarah, this is a really good topic."

And it was then, "Man, do I not see how to do this work!"

But I had learned a lot of the sort of guideposts for thesaurus development in this attempt to understand what were the ways to assemble a multilingual vocabulary. So, the real learning curve working on the *Women's Thesaurus* was what I was alluding to earlier, the syndetic structure; how to conceptually decide what's narrower or broader, what's parallel, where do you want the main term to be, and therefore, which other terms are you going to label as *See*, and the difference between a *see* reference and a *see also* reference. And where do you want to have subheadings or not? Do you want to just create a new main heading or do you want to have *Women* dash something or other?

That is a fundamental philosophical structure of a thesaurus. This is more than you may have wanted to know, but pre-coordinated or post-coordinated vocabulary matters. Do you want the person doing the research, the user, to have to put the words together after the fact? Or do you want your thesaurus to already show what the combinations might be? These structural decisions were very complicated, and I remember spending a lot of time, as a group, working on that and trying to decide on that structure and then, at a certain point it's like, do we have to do this? This is really complicated, but maybe we're making it more complicated than it needs to be. By the time the thesaurus got published, which I think was '94, '92.

Belantara: I think it was 1987.

Pritchard: Was it that early? Not long after the thesaurus was published, and it had a big impact, we had a lot of publishing parties. We sent it to all kinds of publishers and, of course, the Library of Congress and centers, but pretty quickly, in the early nineties emerged, not just the Internet, but very powerful search engines. Even before Google we had Yahoo, we had Mosaic.[14] And I was very skeptical as a librarian: "Oh, that's not good enough, you need subject taxonomies, you need structured searching."

Well, all of us pretty much had to admit that users weren't going to put up with fussing with structured searching. So, I think probably within ten years after it was published, the thesaurus became less necessary because you could rely on new free text searching capabilities, and you could import a search engine from Google to search your own cataloging. You didn't even have to develop your own search software.

We were trying not to duplicate existing indexing languages, or thesauri; we didn't want to just recreate the Library of Congress subject headings, we wanted to really focus on the distinctive language, the distinctive terminology. And we looked a lot at: What were the collections in the different centers? What language was needed? What were those broad subject areas?

Belantara: I just want to go back to what you were saying, you know, about trying to decide on the syndetic structure. Were there any disagreements? And how were they handled when creating the thesaurus, when making those decisions?

Pritchard: I don't recall how we handled the disagreements, but there certainly were disagreements. Maybe we all just made Mary Ellen the chief decider. I don't remember whether that was in fact how we did it. And disagreements were not unpleasant. These were complexities of terminology. It's like, well what do we like better? What's a more common

---

14. Mosaic was among the first web browsers to integrate text and images. It was introduced by the National Center for Supercomputing Applications in 1993. The browser was discontinued in 1997.

term? What's a newer term? So, we struggled with some of the areas, but I don't remember it being confrontational. A lot of it was sort of by consensus, common sense. It's like, look, okay, this is the better term. This is the one that's more frequent in the literature right now, or this is the one on the list from this center and they really are the experts in this field. So, we're going to use their term. I'm trying to recall, and I frankly don't recall; it's just faded in my memory whether we ever had a really difficult, like how are we going to decide?

Here's correspondence between Mary Ellen and the Library of Congress in 1987 as we were trying to get them to use the book. I'm finding that we had developed, internally, some of our own guidelines for a thesaurus structure that we adhered to as a group. I can't tell who wrote these ten-page guidelines for thesaurus structure. And then we had forms that we used when we wanted to submit terms. We worked with international centers because they were also developing thesauri.

Almost every memo I have is signed by Mary Ellen in terms of the international database project and working with a couple of women's centers—one in England, one in the Netherlands—that were also developing thesauri. The ACRL Women's Studies Discussion Group helped with a lot of the testing. By then it was not just the individual librarians on the core thesaurus committee, but larger subject groups. We had a roster of people for the subject groups that was all these librarians. And I was in one subject area communications, I didn't even remember that, but we had the language and literature group, the social science group, and there was a group of about twenty-five librarians in these subject areas. That wasn't the steering committee, but that was really how we worked on the subjects, and the subject groups worked, often individually, with the centers in that early group.

At least one person has passed away by now: Joan Marshall, who was very prominent in the cataloging world. Earnstein Dukes was early on very involved with this; she's now another ARL director. Also, Sara Whaley, who published *Women's Studies Abstracts*, was another great resource (there's an award named after her given by the NWSA). But again, almost all the correspondence I have is going through Mary Ellen, and then these subject groups; I'd sort of forgotten about that, that we did guidelines and we farmed out to ourselves a broader amount of work.

Belantara: What were some of the new terms that were introduced via thesaurus? Could you tell us about any terms that were particularly meaningful to you or the communities you worked with?

Pritchard: Well, the one that always stuck in my mind is what I mentioned earlier, *Looksism*. Because, at that point, I personally had not seen it before, and it came out of a lot of activist feminist activist work and I was just fascinated with that concept. There were probably many other terms that were new to the broader field, but maybe not new to me because I was so immersed in the literature of the time, and not only as a librarian, but my own personal reading.

For instance, I was an early subscriber to *off our backs*, which was published in Washington DC, and if you read that every month, you were just immersed, in the 1970s, in a lot of terminology that, by the time we worked on the thesaurus, probably didn't seem that new to me. But by now I have been away from the field for long enough that I can't remember what was new, and then the language has continued to evolve. So, looking at that snapshot of time in the 1980s, I'm not recalling.

Belantara: So, another question that we had for you: What role do you think race and class difference played in the creation of this thesaurus and how did you think about incorporating cultural differences in the selected terminology?

Pritchard: We were as aware as we could be at that time in the evolution of feminist thought, which was to say somewhat. I would call it, by today's standards, not enough. But we were aware, especially because of having these international partners in other countries, we were aware deeply of the need not to be too ethnocentric in our use of terminology. And we were aware of overtly racist terminology. I don't think we were as well informed about the subtleties. Intersectionality was not yet a word, but it was already a concept. So, in the women's studies field, the phrasing we used at the time was race, sex, and class; race, sex, and class; we have to look at race, sex, and class.

We were definitely aware of that, but maybe not as sophisticated when it came to terminology. We were very aware of how bad were the Library of Congress Subject Headings for both race and sex, especially in very overt kinds of terminology. The classism dimension probably took more of a role in terms of international development in those years; again, because of the UN Decade, not to be underestimated, the awareness of the status of women internationally and how much country-specific norms came to play in different modes of feminist activism and that a feminist group in the US couldn't just assume that its ideas would be welcome in another country.

We were very highly aware of that in that time, and there was a lot of effort made to be sensitive to cultural norms because those conferences were bringing people together from so many different countries. There was a real reckoning among activists that no, you can't just import that concept to this other country and those people might have a different view. So, there was quite a lot of discussion of cultural norms of sexism to a degree; racism, that is as far as it was something that we could see, was an overtly bad word, but did we have a lens literally on every single word? Did we second guess and ask ourselves what are the implications of this word in an intersectional environment? I don't recall that discussion, but many of those concepts sort of permeated.

As I said initially, we did as well as we could do at the time, but we probably were still somewhat elitist, frankly, because most of us came from university institutions and even the women's centers who were members of the National Council, this was not the grassroots women's crisis center in a town or the shelter for battered women. That was where folks were doing everything they could just to fund crisis situations. The centers that were members of the Council were academic centers at universities or independent research centers affiliated with foundations, and so the centers themselves were already coming from a position of privilege, even though we were desperately trying to reach beyond that.

Belantara: Thank you. And then, now I just want to come back briefly to the different categories that were selected in order to structure the thesaurus. I won't read them all, but just to give you a little sampling to refresh your memory, they were: *Communications; Economics and employment; Education; History and social change; International women; Language, literature, religion and philosophy;* and so on. Do you know how these were decided upon?

Pritchard: Nope.

Belantara: And what do you think about these categories today?

Pritchard: I think perhaps these categories derived from literally the way library collections were organized, like Class P was *Literature* and Q was *Sciences*. We may have been just thinking about how did our own libraries, clusters emerge. Although that isn't true of all these categories because some of these span quite broad areas of a library. But I suspect it was based partly on what are the general groupings that we as librarians saw and what are the groupings that were emerging from the women's centers themselves, the lists that they sent, and the sense of importance from the women's centers.

Most women's centers were not collecting heavily in science and technology, most of the collecting was in health. The women's health movement was huge. So, you're not going to see a lot in here about other areas like physics or something, or *Women as physicists* might have been something that would've been focused on under employment and not under science and technology. I think the groupings were just based on our common awareness of the growth of the field, not only in women's studies but in the type of work happening in university library collections.

I'm realizing as I look at the list of who did what subject that I was in the communications list, and I remember deep constant work with one of the other women in that group who published *Media Report to Women*;[15] she was this really dynamic, slightly eccentric activist named Donna

---

15. *Media Report to Women* was founded in 1972 to address the representation of women's lives and experiences in journalism and entertainment. It is currently published

Allen, Dr. Donna Allen.[16] She always made sure to call herself that. The *Media Report to Women* was practically produced in her basement, and she was hugely productive in linking with international issues. She really broke the news to the US about female genital circumcision, for example. All of this came out in the *Media Report to Women* back in the day. She was also based in DC. So, communication was something I worked on a lot because I could get together with Donna. She always was coming over to the Library of Congress, and she introduced me to a lot of people in that State Department public policy world. I imagine this happened in some of the other groups that brought together a librarian and person from a women's center.

Now I'm sheepishly embarrassed to admit that the three people in the communications group were Donna Allen, myself, and Sarah Sherman, who was then the women's studies specialist right here at Northwestern University. So, talk about coming full circle! I certainly remember working very closely with both Sarah Sherman and Donna Allen, but each group was its own little pod. I don't remember a lot of concern that, oh, we've left something out. It was like, well, maybe we'll just send this list over to the such-and-such group. It was really just a way to do the initial stages of the work because once we had developed these groupings, then we moved toward how to consolidate the whole thing.

Belantara: How did the task force actually decide when the thesaurus was complete and what was the feeling or atmosphere once it was sent off for publication?

---

by Communication Research Associates and is available online: http://www.communication-research.org/media-report-to-women/.

16. Allen was an activist from an early age, organizing with farm workers and the American Federation of Labor. In the 1950s, her involvement with the League of Women Voters included opposition to loyalty oaths proposed by the Truman administration. In 1965 Allen refused to testify at a hearing of the House Un-American Activities Committee and was held in contempt of Congress, fined $100, and sentenced to a four-month suspended prison sentence. Allen had a PhD from Howard University and taught in the School of Industrial and Labor Relations at Cornell University.

Pritchard: I don't remember how we decided it was complete. That may again have been Mary Ellen having to just bring down the gavel. I think we always assumed it would be revised, too, which I don't think it ever has been. But I think at the time we thought, well, you know, we've completed it enough, we should go for it. There was an enormous sense of elation when we knew that it had been sent to the publisher. Actually, we were hugely elated when we realized what a good publisher… that it was going to come out from Oxford. It's like we couldn't have wished for a better success path, and as I'm looking now at the list of subject groupings, who was in which subject, literally the individual roster.

I'm realizing that I wasn't actually on the steering committee and that may have been why my memory's a little Swiss cheesy because I felt as if I was, but I'm remembering, well, no, I wasn't. It was Mary Ellen Capek; a great librarian from Colorado called Barbara Parker; and Cheryl Sloan, who was then the librarian at the Business and Professional Women's Foundation (BPW) in DC. The BPW was a really interesting boundary crossing group that started out very conventional, sort of like the League of Women Voters or something. It emerged from the early women's suffrage era almost. And it was early equity advocacy for women in the professions and in business. And it took on quite a feminist tinge in the eighties and it had a very active library, and it really was able to bridge both the audiences.

This was something one was often very aware of in those years: the professional women audience; the activist audience; the scholar audience; and the public policy political audience. These were four quite different segments of audiences in a city like Washington DC. We had all of them, but the different centers didn't always address all of them. So, the National Council and Mary Ellen were, independently of the librarians, connected, not only to the centers, but to these various agencies that worked on women's educational advocacy or women's public policy advocacy. It was a blending of areas of expertise that I think was quite rare.

Drabinski: You've suggested in this interview that the era of free text searching and algorithmic retrieval makes projects like the *Women's Thesaurus* less necessary. Can you say more about that? Do you see any role for these kinds of projects in the contemporary environment?

Pritchard: I definitely still see a role, and I guess what I would say is not less necessary but less urgent. There was literally no way to connect all these centers, databases, and library collections. So, there was a feeling of urgency about, literally, linking the databases and the ability to link different databases, and the ability to search just became easier with various Internet search tools, even in the late nineties, although not as good as it is now. We didn't have metadata crosswalking back then, but, I mean, we still made a huge leap with the advent of the Internet, and not only free text searching, but the ability to upload little local databases and have them available to other people.

What is still extremely important is good tagging, and even though we don't use static, pre-coordinated, structured terminology, we still do huge amounts of metadata tagging. And it's even more important when you have Google searching the metadata that you don't even see on webpages, you know, now we call it search engine optimization. There are people who are employed doing nothing but search engine optimization, and really what that means is adding more tags so that your content gets found on the Internet. And search engine optimization can be kind of done in a lazy way by just pulling terminology out of whatever document you're trying to upload or whatever website you're designing. But you can also optimize that searching by actual explicit tagging of documents, especially for archival materials where the original item might have been in very old-fashioned language.

If you are in an archive right now and you're looking at the records of some women's group from the 1920s and you're digitizing and uploading that, free text searching is not going to make all the linkages you need because people view those issues now with an additional layer of terminology. Or you might actually need to cross reference some rather antiquated term that was being used at the time. If you look at something, for example, like the birth control movement, you know, people were very oblique about what they called it. And if you are looking at the Margaret Sanger archives and all these letters written to her by private individuals, they're not going to say things like, you know, "Hey, I really need birth control," you know. They write in a very indirect fashion using a lot of metaphors and workarounds if you will.

So, the need for enhancing the description of materials as we put materials on the Internet, you can't just scan and do free text searches. You can, but that is only scratching the surface of access. We still have the problem of multilingual access. If you have all kinds of U.S. documents going up and you want to reach out to an international audience, you're putting a huge burden on them if you don't try to broaden your tagging or have some cross-walking with lists from other countries.

IFLA [International Federation of Library Associations] for a while really picked up on some of this work, and there was a women's interest group within IFLA that looked at a lot of international database access. I don't know if that's still happening. But, so yes, I still think there's a need, but it's labor intensive to do this kind of tagging. And so smaller women's centers might not worry about it as much, but I think major research centers really trying to improve access should still be thinking about how to enhance their tagging and how to have less sexist terminology. Don't just default to that Library of Congress Subject Heading list, which still has an awful lot of *Women in*, *Women as*, or *Women something* the qualifier. Adding a qualifier to a word automatically reduces the importance.

If you say women in business, that's not as important as saying business owners. You don't want to have to say women business owners. That's a denigration, if you will. There's been very interesting studies by a linguist, a very feminist linguist, a man called George Lakoff, that showed how denigrating it is when you have to add extra words to a term that means it's no longer the main thing. It's sort of like the margin instead of the center, which we've often talked about in feminist studies. If you want to center women, you don't want to have to use all kinds of add-on terminology.

Drabinski: We have one last technical question. In speaking with Mary Ellen, she indicated that the Library of Congress added the *Women's Thesaurus* to its official MARC code list of the thesaurus.

Pritchard: Yes, I just was looking at that letter.

Drabinski: Do you know how this generally is decided? Having worked with LOC, are the groups involved in these thesauri consulted, and how did you feel about that inclusion?

Pritchard: We were very excited at that inclusion. I knew from working in the Library of Congress that there was, as I was saying earlier, a very elaborate process for proposing a new subject heading. Every week there was a meeting in the subject cataloging division of the senior subject catalogers who would review the proposals for new headings. And it took years for the reference librarians to be allowed to even sit in as observers in that meeting, let alone we were never allowed initially to actually propose headings.

So, it was a very tightly controlled process for proposing and reviewing headings. And there was an official list of additional thesauri that were considered valid for consulting to either agree that yes, we should add this heading to the Library of Congress subject headings, or we should use their term. Just because a term was listed somewhere didn't mean the Library of Congress would consider it worthy or have credibility. So, to be added to the list of approved thesauri, and I'm looking at this memo from Mary Ellen, September, 1989, all its one line, "Hey, we are getting mainstreamed, how about that?" And it's attached to the letter from actually not even just the chief of subject cataloging, but the chief of the MARC standards office.

The MARC cataloging was very tightly controlled. In the MARC bibliographic record for a book or for a subject heading, you had to enter what was the source of your subject heading. If you didn't use the Library of Congress Subject Headings, could you use MeSH, Medical Subject Headings? Could you use, and there was a list of what were approved to

TO: Sarah, Pat and Sue
FROM: Mary Ellen
DATE: September 14, 1989

Hey--we are getting mainstreamed. How about that?

The Sara Delano Roosevelt Memorial House/47-49 East 65th Street/New York, N.Y. 10021/(212) 570-5001

Figure 7. NCRW cover memo, 1989, from *Women's Thesaurus* editor, Mary Ellen Capek reflecting on the Library of Congress' assignment of the code "wot" for use in MARC catalog records.

be entered into the MARC record and you needed a code. When we were granted this code, WOT could be in the subfield two of the 6XX subject headings. So the 650s, for example—this is cataloger speak—were where you would list your subject headings. And if you didn't use the official ones, you could use alternative ones if they were approved alternatives.

Now, you could use your own but then your record wouldn't get used by anybody else. If you uploaded a record to OCLC and another library was going to use it, they would look in that field to see whether your subject headings were sort of valid or just fringy. So, to be designated an official code for the *Women's Thesaurus* meant that anybody who used those headings had a leg up getting their bibliographic catalog entry able to be shared with credibility. Again, it was all about credibility.

You could have used those headings, but someone would not have necessarily used your cataloging record; they would've gone ahead and redone it with other headings. But once the thesaurus became an official source, then if you listed that in the MARC record with that code that meant that somebody wouldn't have to redo the cataloging work. So, it was a huge ease for catalogers in other libraries to know that the *Women's Thesaurus* was one of the official source books for subject headings. And it was one of the outside, non-LC librarians who was part of our group that wrote to the Library of Congress an official request to request this. One of the things I found while working at the Library of Congress is that it was often better for a librarian on the outside to write and request these than for me on the inside.

Belantara: What do you think about the *Women's Thesaurus* project now? Would you have any advice for somebody taking on this type of project?

Pritchard: It was a very exciting project to be part of. We really felt like we were doing something, and not only were we doing something, we were crossing professional boundaries as well as obviously disciplinary ones. But it felt so meaningful to bring together scholars, librarians, people administering women's centers, and funders. And my feeling was that although it was very linked to a certain moment in time, it was very valuable for, in a permanent way, for showing the possibility that cross-functional work and the benefit of linking the people who understand the tools, the people who understand the domain, and the people who understand the sort of policy that has to go into this.

And that's what I would urge people looking at projects like this today. Any kind of project related to developing resources, you've got to have the people who understand how those resources are used and needed, and then what are the organizations and tools that you need to make it happen. You can't take a narrow view. As I said, I don't think this particular project would happen today, partly because there were fewer rigid boundaries back then among women's organizations. You could drop in and out of a lot of these organizations and everybody was very welcoming. We didn't have as detailed an array of organizations, so there were fewer places to go to work on things, and so it was easier to converge everybody in a sense. It also took a huge amount of energy from literally one woman to really push it through. And thus, you need a combination of a very outcome-driven leader and then a big team that is committed to the vision of that. I don't think either could have done it without the other.

Drabinski: Thank you so much, Sarah for that.

Pritchard: And I want to thank both of you for doing this. It really refreshed a lot of my memories of what we were doing back then and why we were so energized.

The Homosaurus

Introduction

In 1982, Jack van der Wel, a founder of Homodok, a collection of LGBT materials at the University of Amsterdam, published a bibliographic database to archive their collections. Recognizing that existing vocabularies such as the Library of Congress Subject Headings were insufficient, the collection was described using a homegrown Queer Thesaurus, a collection of terms that were specific to experiences of, and research into, homosexuality. That same year in Leeuwarden, the Anna Blamanhuis library was established to collect diverse, multicultural materials related to queer life, described using a term list of their own. Each of these vocabularies expanded as their collections expanded, with significant growth in the Queer Thesaurus in 1987 due to the automation of indexing at Homodok. In 1993, the two institutions merged term lists. Six years later, Homodok merged with a collection of lesbian materials held at Anna Blamanhuis to become the Internationaal Homo/Lesbisch Informatiescentrum en Archief (IHLIA) LGBTI Heritage, a repository of materials that embraced the broad diversity of the LGBT community. The merged term lists became the *Homosaurus*.

In 2013, recognizing the need for a formal thesaurus rather than a simple list of terms, van der Wel worked with Ellen Greenblatt, a librarian in the U.S., to turn the list of terms into a formal print thesaurus using a hierarchical and syndetic structure. The resulting print version of the *Homosaurus* was made available to LGBTQ+ archives and documentation centers across the world. K.J. Rawson, founder of the Digital Transgender Archive (DTA), turned to the *Homosaurus* to describe this growing collection. Working in a digital environment, Rawson suspected that the *Homosaurus* would be even more valuable as an online linked open data vocabulary. The structure of linked open data enables terms to be applied and located in a diversity of web environments. He reached out to van der Wel and the two of them worked to transform the print version into the first version of *Homosaurus* as a linked data project. In 2016, Rawson and van der Wel established an editorial board to oversee ongoing changes. The board instituted a revision process that narrowed the *Homosaurus* by excluding terms that were not specific to LGBTQ+ experience. This change was revelatory for the editorial board, since this enabled them to focus on describing their world and not the whole world. The thesaurus is currently governed by a nine-person editorial board chaired at the time of this volume's writing by K.J. Rawson, Associate Professor of English and Women's, Gender, and Sexuality Studies at Northeastern University. *Homosaurus* has been assigned a code for use in Library of Congress catalog records. The *Homosaurus* is continually revised and updated, and a Spanish version is under development. The most current version at the time of this writing was published in June 2023.

Homosaurus Timeline

1982 Homodok bibliographic database released
Homodok, a research collection of LGBT materials held at the University of Amsterdam, debuts its bibliographic database. The database was indexed using the Queer Thesaurus, a set of terms developed internally to describe the collection.

1982 Anna Blamanhuis founded
The Anna Blamanhuis in Leeuwarden, the Netherlands. A multicultural lesbian and gay information center, the organization intentionally collected materials from diverse parts of the community. Materials were described using an internal word list.

1987 Queer Thesaurus expanded
Automation enables Jack van der Wel and colleagues to greatly expand

terms related to sexuality, sexual techniques, and sexual object choice for materials in the Homodok collections.

1993 Homodok and Anna Blamanhuis merge terms
The terms from Homodok are merged with those from the Anna Blamanhuis to produce an expanded Queer Thesaurus.

1999 IHLIA is founded
Homodok and the Lesbian Archives of Leeuwarden, held at the Anna Blamanhuis, merge to become the Internationaal Homo/Lesbisch Informatiecentrum en Archiel (IHLIA). Materials are described using the combined wordlists, now known as *Homosaurus*.

2013 *Homosaurus* transformed to inclusive and hierarchical thesaurus
Van der Wel and U.S. librarian Ellen Greenblatt produce the first major revision of the *Homosaurus*, adding hundreds of new terms and implementing a syndetic, hierarchical thesaurus structure.

2015 *Homosaurus* becomes online linked data vocabulary
K.J. Rawson uses *Homosaurus* terms to index holdings in the Digital Transgender Archive. Recognizing the value of the vocabulary for online LGBTQIA+ projects, he begins collaborating with van der Wel to transform the *Homosaurus*.

2016 *Homosaurus* editorial board established
Rawson and van der Wel establish the *Homosaurus* editorial board. The group decides to remove general terms from the vocabulary, resulting in a narrower vocabulary confined to LGBTQ-specific terms.

2019 *Homosaurus* version 2 released

2021 *Homosaurus* version 3 released

K.J. Rawson on the Homosaurus

Biography

K.J. Rawson is an Associate Professor of English and Women's, Gender, and Sexuality Studies at Northeastern University, where he also co-directs the NULab for Texts, Maps, and Networks. He works at the intersections of the Digital Humanities and Rhetoric, LGBTQ+, and Feminist Studies. Focusing on archives as key sites of cultural power, he studies the rhetorical work of queer and transgender archival collections in brick-and-mortar and digital spaces. Rawson is founder and director of the Digital Transgender Archive, an award-winning collection of trans-related historical materials, and he chairs the editorial board of the *Homosaurus*, an LGBTQ+ linked data vocabulary.

About the Interview

The following transcribed interview of K.J. Rawson took place on August 1st, 2022, as part of the *Ways of Knowing Oral History Project*. The interview was auto transcribed and then edited by Amanda Belantara and Emily Drabinski. Care was taken to not alter the original transcription's contents. However, the editors have formatted the following to improve readability and provided footnotes for clarity where appropriate. The original transcript and recording can be accessed through the *Ways of Knowing Oral History Project* held at NYU Libraries.[1]

Transcript from the *Ways of Knowing Oral History Project*

Interviewee: K.J. Rawson, Chair of the *Homosaurus* Editorial Board, Director of the Digital Transgender Archive, Associate Professor of English and Women's, Gender and Sexuality Studies, Northeastern University.
Interviewers: Emily Drabinski & Amanda Belantara
Date: Aug 1, 2022
Location: Virtual Interview; Northeastern University

Emily Drabinski: Today we're interviewing K.J. Rawson, Associate Professor of English and Women's Gender and Sexuality studies at Northeastern University and Chair of the *Homosaurus* Editorial Board. The interview was conducted for the *Ways of Knowing Oral History Project*. The interview took place virtually on August 1st, 2022, recorded locally by Kip Clark at K.J.'s office in Boston, Massachusetts. The interviewers are Amanda Belantara and Emily Drabinski based in New York City.

Drabinski: K.J., can you tell us a bit about your background and education?

---

1. Rawson's recording is available here: https://search.library.nyu.edu/permalink/01NYU_INST/1d6v258/alma990098389960107871.

K.J. Rawson: Sure. I guess the best place to start would be my undergraduate studies. I started to find my love of language, in particular, throughout my time in undergraduate. I was an English major at Cornell and what I especially loved about becoming an English major was the small classrooms, the falling in love with books alongside other people, getting to chat with other folks about it, and really wrangle with language, with what was happening on the page, how it made us feel, and the work that it was doing in the world.

After I finished my undergraduate degree, I didn't want be done. I didn't have other really specific intentions beyond that, but I knew I didn't want to finish these kinds of conversations. So, I went to graduate school and I got a master's in English literature, in part out of inertia. I loved having those continuing conversations, but I wanted to really find a space where I could look more at the way language was working in the world, the impacts that it was having in persuasive discourse, not just in aesthetic and literary forms. And so that's how I found my way to rhetoric.

Once I finished that Master's Degree, I went on to get my PhD in Rhetoric. At that point, I got a chance to really focus on how queer history and queer language was impacting people—researchers, but also the general public and the ways that queer language was circulating in the world. And it was that background that brought me to the *Homosaurus* Project and also brought me to the Digital Transgender Archive,[2] which is another project that I direct.

Drabinski: Can you tell us a bit about your professional position right now?

Rawson: Right now I am at Northeastern University. My home department is an English department, and I also am jointly appointed in Wom-

---

2. The Digital Transgender Archive (DTA) is housed at Northeastern University and serves as "an online hub for digitized historical materials, born-digital materials, and information on archival holdings throughout the world." It is available online at https://www.digitaltransgenderarchive.net.

en's, Gender, and Sexuality Studies. I also co-direct a digital humanities and social science and computational social science initiative here called the NULab. Through all of these various channels, I get a chance to have colleagues and collaborators from different parts of the university, which has been a really perfect way of tapping into all of my interests and getting to meet with folks who do lots of similar work.

Drabinski: When did you first get involved with the *Homosaurus* Project?

Rawson: My *Homosaurus* involvement started in 2015. I came across the *Homosaurus* because I had a problem. I was just starting the Digital Transgender Archive at the time, and I was having a terrible time finding good subject terms to describe the materials we were starting to process for the Digital Trans Archive. I was looking to the Library of Congress Subject Headings and really not finding what I needed.

The Digital Trans Archive, as you can anticipate, is full of queer and trans materials and things that were not adequately described by existing controlled vocabularies. I think I read about the *Homosaurus* first on conference proceedings… maybe from one of the earliest GLBT Archives, Libraries, Museums, and Special Collections (ALMS) conferences. I think there was an early presentation on the *Homosaurus* there. So, I tracked down Jack van der Wel's email address and just reached out cold and said, "Hey, this sounds cool."

At that point, in 2015, he sent me a Word doc version of the *Homosaurus*, which is what it had been, from my understanding, for its first few decades. I got that and I said, "Oh, this is incredible."

It really gave me a lot of hope that there was a controlled vocabulary out there that could work within the Digital Trans Archive that I was trying to use it within.

Drabinski: In 2015 when you're first encountering the *Homosaurus*, can you tell us a little bit about the social and political environment that you were in? What was happening around that time?

Rawson: It's funny, it's seven years ago, so it both feels like a long time ago, but then also, it feels like we're in the same moment in many ways. What seems to have changed since then is that trans communities, in particular, have become far more of a political and legislative focus in not-so-great ways.

At the time it felt more like what we were doing was under the radar. Especially with the Digital Trans Archive, it felt like a somewhat obscure project or at least a niche project. We knew that there would be great demand for it, but that that demand would be fairly specific and really tailored to trans communities ourselves. But that has really changed a lot and I think that, even for the *Homosaurus* as well, there's so much, not only greater attention to LGBTQ+ resources and information landscapes, but I also think that we're seeing a lot of attention to activism around metadata and reparative descriptive practices.

Projects like the *Homosaurus* are starting to gain a lot of attention in a way that I don't think I saw as much promise for in 2015. I actually see the difference as one of capacity building and expansion from where we are and, I think, where we're heading in the next five to ten years.

Drabinski: To zoom out a bit and talk about the *Homosaurus*… the initial vocabulary emerges in the 1980s at Homodok at the University of Amsterdam. How did this Dutch project come to the attention of information workers in the United States?

Rawson: I'm not sure if I'm the best person to answer that question. I know that Ellen Greenblatt was at the center of some of that work, but I don't know much beyond that. I know that Jack and Ellen, in particular, directly collaborated on that project and it had been translated, I believe, either with Ellen's input or just before Ellen got involved. And then I know that Ellen worked a lot on expanding the vocabulary. I think that was also the moment where it transformed from a flat listing to a hierarchical thesaurus. There was a pretty significant ontological shift at that point, as well, and I believe that was in the late 1990s, but I'm not quite sure when those conversations started or how they happened.

Drabinski: Can you tell us a bit more about that transition? What is the difference between the flat Word document that you received and what Ellen did with the project?

Rawson: Actually, the Word document was still in existence through the early 2010s, so through 2015. But what happened with the vocabulary is that, initially, it was just a listing of terms that were not put in relation to one another. So, it was just an alphabetical list of terms in isolation from one another. And it was in the 1990s—again, to the best of my knowledge—that they were put into a hierarchy format. There were relationships that were built out. Some terms became broader terms, some were narrower, and then others were put as related terms, which is more of a horizontal relationship.

Drabinski: Do you know when the *Homosaurus* was translated into English?

Rawson: That was in the 1990s, to the best of my knowledge, but it has maintained an active Dutch and English translation since then. Jack has continued to translate every term that we have added since then.

Drabinski: Can you tell us who was involved in the translation to English initially?

Rawson: I wish I could, but again, Ellen's name is the only one who I know from the English side of things who was contributing.

Drabinski: You talked a bit about your first encounter with the *Homosaurus*. Can you tell us in a little more detail about that initial encounter? A little more about what you're hoping to use the vocabulary for and some of your initial reactions?

Rawson: I just remember working with students in a lab. This was when I was a faculty member at the College of the Holy Cross in Worcester, Massachusetts, so even our conversations themselves...let's just say we always had a closed door. And so, we would be looking at these historical artifacts and some of the earliest materials we processed were program guides from Fantasia Fair from the 1970s and 1980s.[3] We had a few runs of fantastic community publications, things like *Transgender Tapestry,*[4] *Drag* magazine,[5] these fabulous and rich historical artifacts, and we would be seeking out language to add to that.

Of course, my students who are digital natives were like, "we'll just add our own tags to it."

And I would say, "Well, wait a minute here. Though this is a joyfully queer project, I do think there is some benefit in having a controlled set of terms."

We would have these long conversations about the philosophy behind that and the meeting of queer theory and the practice of digital archiving. Though I'm certainly committed to the endless proliferation of language, and I am someone who loves language theory, I do think that there is a real practical value in having a set list of terms to apply in information environments so that people can better discover resources. As soon as I found the *Homosaurus*, I saw this rich and incredible potential and I thought, "Oh, this is great. We can start describing these materials much better."

But then, of course, immediately I'm like, "Oh no, that's not good." Or, "that term is really out of date."

It was at once this beautiful resource that wonderfully supplemented and pushed back, in some ways, against LCSH, but then on the other

---

3. Fantasia Fair was an annual gathering in Provincetown, Massachusetts, for "crossdressers and transsexuals." The first Fantasia Fair was held in 1975. The event continues to be held each year under the name Transweek. Further history can be found at https://transweek.org/40-years-of-history/.

4. *Transgender Tapestry* was a magazine by and for the trans community published from 1979 to 2008. Holding at DTA can be accessed here: https://www.digitaltransgenderarchive.net/col/7w62f824d.

5. *Drag* was a magazine about drag queens published in the 1970s and 1980s. Holdings at DTA can be accessed here: https://www.digitaltransgenderarchive.net/col/6682x401g.

hand, it was really imperfect and also needed some TLC. It was maybe two months after I had initially received the Word doc that I reached back out to Jack and tentatively said, "Hey, what would you think about setting up an editorial board?"

Of course, I was a bit timid about it because I had just found out about this project, and here I am trying to basically elbow my way in and say, "Hey, let's make it better" to one of the people who had been around since the '80s and who had been working on it for more than thirty years at that point. But to Jack's credit, he was enthusiastic about the idea.

Drabinski: Can you tell us a bit about how you assembled that first *Homosaurus* editorial board?

Rawson: That first six months or so, it really was a lot of Jack and I reaching out to anyone we knew who might be interested. We were hitting up anyone that we knew of that we thought could be interested. Emily, I'm surprised if we didn't reach out to you, actually.

Drabinski: I think you did reach out to me, and I connected you to Amber Billey [a member of the *Homosaurus* board].

Rawson: Perfect, so you are part of this history as well. I'm curious now, and I really want to look back to see if that was the first time that I had met with Amber Billey, but I certainly knew Billey's name before that in any case. I think the initial board was eight people and there was great energy at that very first meeting. It was a group of folks who are passionate about queer information, and I remember us giggling already in our first meeting, and I just knew this was going to be a great group of folks. And in fact, almost all of the original board has remained to this day. We did lose Cat Walker a few years back and he was one of our founding editorial board members. But it's just been a dynamic and energized group that has remained a dynamic and energized group to this day.

Drabinski: Where was the first meeting held?

Rawson: Virtually. We were doing Zoom meetings before it was the Zoom meeting landscape that we have now. In fact, I think we tried out every remote meeting platform that is in existence. We did every different kind, and it was almost a running joke because we could never find the right links. We would switch almost month-to-month when we were meeting to try out different platforms because they weren't working well for us. I'd say that more than half of the board I have still never met in person, though we've been working together for six years now.

Figure 8. The *Homosaurus* Editorial Board meets on Zoom. Top row, L to R: Bri Watson, K.J. Rawson, Jay Colbert; second row, L to R: Clair Kronk (former board member), Adrian Williams, Jack van der Wel; third row, L to R: Billey Albina, Chloe Noland, Janaya Kizzie; bottom row, L to R: Marika Cifor, Keahi Ka'iwalani Adolpho.

Drabinski: Can you tell us who is on the current editorial board and a bit about your goals?

Rawson: Sure, so, the current editorial board: I've already mentioned Amber Billey, who's still on the board; Marika Cifor, Jay Colbert, Janaya Kizzie, Claire Kronk, Chloe Noland, myself, Bri Watson, Jack van der Wel, who I've also talked a lot about, and Adrian Williams. So, it's a good-sized board. We actually hear from folks really frequently who want to join the board, and it's often a challenging position for us to be in because again, we want to support this project's growth and really make sure that we can make it into the best resource possible. But it's really hard to figure out the exact balance and the number of folks on any given board and organization. We've tried to keep the number around ten. We've had a few folks who come on and off over the years, but that seems to be the sweet spot for us. It's nice that we're now in a position where everyone keeps coming to us, rather than us having to try to beg folks to join onto this project that they had never heard about before.

Drabinski: And what are the goals of the board?

Rawson: We call ourselves an editorial board and I think that's an apt title, although I think it under-accounts for all the work that is happening by the board. Our primary job is to maintain the vocabulary, to review new changes, to spearhead initiatives, and to develop branches of the vocabulary that follow certain themes. We also do a lot of cleanup work. We still find terms in the vocabulary that we wonder, how did that get there? How come no one ever noticed that before? Or how come this term doesn't have any relationships associated with it? So, there's still a lot of what feels to me like basic maintenance of the vocabulary that we do.

We've had a grant over the past year from Northeastern University, and that has been an incredible opportunity to support a graduate student who's been working on this project throughout the past year. And so we've seen a tremendous amount of growth recently. We've had hundreds of new terms that have been added in the past twelve months, but the editorial board does a lot more than that.

Some of our members do a lot of public speaking and really excel at hosting workshops for libraries that want to implement it, and others are reaching out to archives where this might be a benefit, and so forth. We also have some of our members who are great at fostering collaborations with other organizations and so they might reach out to another organization and try to get feedback on certain parts of the vocabulary. These efforts are really important for us because we recognize the limitations of who's on the board at any given time and how the vocabulary itself is reflecting our own areas of expertise. So, we always want to be pushing out and getting input and seeking collaborations to continue to enrich and extend the vocabulary.

Drabinski: How do you feel about the group's composition in terms of race, class, geographic location and how does that impact the thesaurus? You've written a bit about efforts to expand racial diversity on the board. Can you tell us how you're working toward that?

Rawson: Yeah, I'm more than happy to talk about that. One of the things that we joke about a lot as a board is that we have a real over-representation of trans people but some of our trans terms are some of the least developed in our vocabulary. We try to be really attuned to our own gaps and limitations and some of the things that we have not built out as well for the vocabulary. We knew even from the start that it was a significant problem that our board was overwhelmingly white, but several years back we realized that it was a problem we needed to address.

Of course, we're contending with a library and information landscape where that is also largely the case. We made a decision as a board three years ago that we would not bring on any new board members who were white. We just felt like it was unethical to continue building and so dramatically misrepresenting the communities that we were purporting to try to support for information access. Since that time we have recruited several people of color who have joined the board, but I think that, honestly, the people who are on the board are not necessarily working in areas that are aligned with their own identities, which I think speaks to the fact that some of our trans terms are not as well built out as other terms. The way that our vocabulary grows is through our collaborations. One of the collaborations that we have worked on in the past year is with Krü Maekdo, who directs the Black Lesbian Archives,[6] and she has offered a

---

6. Black Lesbian Archives was founded in 2017 as an online hub for collecting materials related to Black lesbian history and experience. The digital collections can be accessed here: https://blacklesbianarchives.wixsite.com/info.

lot of feedback on building out the vocabulary based on what would be supportive for use in a context like the Black Lesbian Archives. We've tried to build and expand based on those kinds of collaborations.

In doing so we've really found that there are so many areas that we are just not attuned to as a board. Someone, for example, pointed out that up until, I think it was a year and a half ago, we didn't even have *gay marriage* in the vocabulary. That's one of those things that we chuckle about because it was just not a priority for anyone on the board. But of course, some of our users were like, "Excuse me, you don't have gay marriage."

We feel like we're always doing what feels like an impossible job of trying to capture this really complex and diverse language and linguistic diversity among queer communities, and we're trying to do the best job that we can, but we always are kind of, at for least me personally, putting this project out there with a bit of a wince because I know that there are parts of it that are just so imperfect. But again, it's still worth putting it out there and continuing to put our effort and our love into it and to try to make it an improved resource.

Drabinski: The board also includes practicing librarians, as well as scholars in the field. Is that mix intentional? Can you tell us how those relationships shape the *Homosaurus* Project?

Rawson: Yes, I think that the relationship of the board members and their various backgrounds and expertise is the most important part of the board. For example, when we lost Cat, he was the person who did the most library cataloging of anyone on our board. And when he passed, not only did we all feel such a tremendous loss of his friendship and his being a close colleague of ours, but we also realized we were missing a really important area of expertise on the board.

About six months later, I reached out to Adrian Williams, who is a metadata librarian at the University of Kentucky, and they do cataloging every day. It was really such a perfect opportunity to seek out someone who also has expertise similar to Cat's because Adrian so often will speak up at board meetings and be like, "No, nope, that's not how we're going to be using that in a library context."

We also have folks who work in archives, and the uses of the *Homosaurus* in archives are often slightly different than in library contexts. Getting all of those voices together in our board has been indispensable to building the vocabulary so that it's a useful resource across these different contexts.

Drabinski: Can you tell us how you work together? How often do you meet? Do you ever meet in person or only online? And how do you stay motivated to continue working on the project?

Rawson: We've never met in person. In fact, some of the folks on the editorial board I have done even closer collaborations with, like writing grants and articles together, and I still haven't met all those folks. We are a board that works well together remotely. Just this past Friday we had a board retreat, so we had a three hour long Zoom meeting together, and I can say that at the end of that retreat there were people who were still lingering at the end of our three hours. We have found this great synergy, even in Zoom. I have to say, it's one of the most enjoyable Zoom meetings that I have.

We meet monthly. These board retreats are a bit of an anomaly for us that we were able to do with the sponsorship of Northeastern University's grant that we're on right now. Normally, we just meet once a month for either an hour or an hour and a half and then we do a lot of communication in between meetings, over email predominantly. When the board meets, we usually have a pretty light agenda—we know we need to look at new terms, we usually will check in about ongoing projects, and then often there'll be either a problem or a proposal about a larger area that will come up. So, we might tackle something like acronyms—how are we going to handle acronyms as a vocabulary?

As you can imagine, that's one of those ones that can be really tough for us—to figure out how to both normalize and support a widespread usage of various iterations of the LGBTQ+ acronym. Those are the kinds of things that we try to balance in every meeting: bigger picture things, but then also specific term approvals. And just like at our very first meeting, we continue to laugh and often giggle at just about every meeting. We also really work well together in shared documents and shared spreadsheets, both in synchronous and asynchronous collaboration. It is often the case that we will all be in a doc together and people will be editing the same sentence and there will be no stepping on toes; there are no hurt feelings. People really seem to be quite generous with co-authorship and co-creation and that has always served the board really well.

Drabinski: Is there ever conflict on the board?

Rawson: We disagree, definitely. I think that that's really important and really healthy. There are certainly times when we will have a different opinion on something, and a couple different folks might go and research it and come back and say, "Oh, I think this would actually be best practice."

And someone else will say, "Oh, actually, based on my research, I think this is best practice."

Then we'll work to find a solution together. To my knowledge anyway, and of course I'd want to ask all of my fellow board members, but I don't think we've experienced many instances where people will end a meeting with hurt feelings or frustrations about how a decision went down. Usually, because we all share an equal passion and commitment to the project, we end up coming to a place of mutual understanding, and there's so much opportunity to build in nuance with related terms if there's a term you really objected to or a scope note you didn't like or something. Usually, most of the board members are like, "Okay, let's work on that until we're all comfortable with it."

There are very few opportunities for someone to really put their foot down and say, "I'm unhappy with this approach," because I think that most of the time, someone will just say, "You know what, I don't see that collaboration or that venture as being as worthwhile as something else, but go ahead, you do it."

It's one of those cases where we will just splinter off and someone can do the work, and then someone else will just step back and work on something else. That's more often the case; there may be a difference of opinion with where we're heading or certain initiatives that we want to put our energies into, but it's never a problem because we can just separate that out and people can do the work and then come back to the board, and it will be supported at the board level.

> *One of the ways that we've thought about the purpose of the* Homosaurus *is to provide more terminology, to make more words available to be used to enhance discoverability.... you're going to have someone coming into a library and searching for that term and how mind-blowing would it be when they actually can find materials related to that term?*

Drabinski: Can you tell us how your work on *Homosaurus* is funded?

Rawson: This grant that we just received from Northeastern University was our first official funding. Prior to that, this project has been a labor of love and something that we've all done on a volunteer basis. It's not an expensive project. I've been able to host the *Homosaurus* through the Digital Trans Archive (DTA) platform up until this past year. Part of what this grant allowed us to do was take the *Homosaurus* out from under the DTA and establish it on its own server space and its own administrative and hosting environment. That was the first time that had been the case.

Prior to that, it was just under the auspices of the DTA. You don't really know that when you're accessing the vocabulary from the front end, so it didn't matter too much. But in terms of opportunities for future grants, that was a really important step for us, to be able to make sure that the projects were disentangled. Also, it really wasn't a sustainable infrastructure for the long term, it was just the way that we could get it set up quickly, to use in the DTA.

I must confess to you that I had absolutely no idea that it meant a lot that we were creating it as a linked data vocabulary back in 2015 when we were doing it because our software developer, Steven Anderson, who's just phenomenal and has supported this project every step of the way, said, "Oh, well, if you're going to use it in the DTA, you can't just use it as an internal and backend-controlled vocabulary. Let's make it a linked data vocabulary and then others can access it."

I was just sort of blithely like, "Sure, whatever, as long as we can use it."

Then we started to get contacted by people who also wanted to access it, and I thought, "Oh, there might be something here."

The amount of usage that we've had since then has just skyrocketed. So, our first set of funding has been really helpful and important in being able to set up the scaffolding for future growth and future funding. Up until this point it's been…I wouldn't even call it shoestring…it's like, bare feet, I guess…there's not even a shoe apparatus. But then this past year, having some grant support has given us the opportunity to really gear up for our future work.

Drabinski: We're interested in the initial decisions you made when you took over the *Homosaurus* as an editorial board. How did you go about getting started with those revisions and do you remember any of the initial decisions you had to make?

Rawson: We actually have our minutes all the way back to the first meeting, so that'd be a fun little research project if someone wanted to go through and read through all of our early conversations. I'd say for the first year, maybe year and a half, we were like a boat going in a circle on a lake. We were definitely revisiting the same conversations over and over again. We were all happy to be out on the lake, but we were, like, what is going on here? What are we doing?

Part of the grappling around that was that the original *Homosaurus* was meant to be a standalone vocabulary, meaning that an archivist could use it to fully describe all of their collections. So, it included lots of LGBTQ+ terms, of course, but also lots of other, broader terms that really weren't LGBTQ specific but that were parent terms for LGBTQ terms. For example, terms like *Performance* or *Family* or *Art*—these broad subject headings. We realized as we were trying to dissect the vocabulary for the first year that we couldn't do a good job treating the *Homosaurus* like a standalone vocabulary because it was just so big.

We kept adding all these new terms and often at a meeting someone would be like, "But how is that queer? What does that have to do with queer people?"

Then we'd say, "Oh, I don't know."

And so, we'd have these conversations, and it took us about a year or a year and a half to really settle on a scope. In that process we determined that we wanted to focus exclusively on queer language and terminology. That was such a moment of clarity for us because we could have kept going around in circles for a long time, but once we decided to do that, the next few meetings we just cut every term that was not sufficiently queer. You could imagine the joy of all these queer librarians and academics just being like, "Nope, not queer enough, not queer enough."

And just deleting, deleting, deleting. We must have deleted hundreds and hundreds of terms—maybe 800 terms were deleted. It was like, whoa, okay, what are we going to have left when we're done with this? But it allowed us to get to the point where we could say, this is something we can do well; this is something that we can develop a niche and an area of expertise in. We know we can't do all the other stuff really well, so let's just try to narrow it even further.

That decision has come to challenge us in some ways still because we want to be able to group terms together. We've sort of gone back against that scope in a few moments when we want it to still be readable to users. But then at the same time, it has really narrowed our focus in such a helpful way and it has allowed us to continue to say, "No, that's not really in the vocabulary, you can find that somewhere else."

But it's also meant that we will often compare a proposal for a new term to existing vocabularies and if we're not finding it anywhere else, we will include it even if it's kind of on the periphery of being LGBTQ+-specific. We will really push our own scope and boundaries if we feel like we can use our linked data environment to support other kinds of information discovery that aren't necessarily within our purview but that we think would be helpful to include.

Drabinski: Can you give an example of one of those terms?

Rawson: For example, we wanted to include critical race theory and intersectionality. Those are terms that are very important to LGBTQ+ communities and discovery, of course, but they wouldn't necessarily fall squarely under the umbrella of an LGBTQ+ vocabulary. But we were, like, those definitely need to be in there, right? These terms need to be made accessible to folks who are using the *Homosaurus*.

Part of the problem is that when we talk about the terms that are in the *Homosaurus* versus ones that aren't, the LCSH is changing rapidly, but it feels to me that it's changing quicker than it ever has. Since I'm not involved in proposing or evaluating new terms for LCHS, I'm completely ignorant of the process. My experience in the past had been that terms were very slow to change, but it seems like there's an increase in speed, at least with queer-related and trans-related terminology. Some of the arguments that we have made in the past about these terms not being available in LCSH, that environment is shifting a bit, but I'm not always as invested in keeping up with it. Though we have a mapping between LCSH and the *Homosaurus*, I think that's only one data point and not necessarily the most interesting one anymore for the project.

Amanda Belantara: Okay, so as we continue talking a little bit about revisions, I just have another follow up question. Could you tell us about any new terms that were introduced via the revision process and were any of those terms particularly meaningful to you? And are discussions related to these changes documented along the way?

Rawson: I'll answer the last part first, which is that we haven't documented the discussions beyond our own minutes and internal documentation, though we have started to produce more public facing works. We have been participating more in public interviews and in having recorded trainings and some academic publications. In those spaces you're starting to see some of our conversations seep out, and you get more of a sense of what the back end of the project looks like. One of the things that I think has been really interesting about the changes we've made over the past year is that we have not been shy about making really big changes. That can be something that's really intimidating, especially with an all-volunteer project because you see a change or a proposal and you think, "Oh, that's a great idea, but gosh, who is going to do that work?"

You could just see the number of hours in front of you for how long it will take to implement a proposal, and so the nice and beautiful thing about this past year is that we've had a funded graduate student who has been able to support this project. That's Caitlin Roles and they have not shied away from these big changes either. For example, one of our collaborators whom I've already been talking about, Krü Maekdo, noticed maybe a year ago that the *Homosaurus* had all of our race-related terms as second within a term string. For example, it would be *Lesbian Black people*. It would always be the queer term, the race or ethnicity term, and then the person term. What that did was, it prioritized the LGBTQ identity. One of the first things that Krü said was, like, "No, no, no. I would actually always include the race or ethnicity term first." That was a proposal we brought back to the board and the board was immediately like, "Yep, that sounds great, let's do that."

That was a huge change. I mean, the number of terms that then had to change as a result of that was incredible, but it was a really important change for the project. That's the kind of thing that we really have been able to take on and to face and to implement because we have grant funding in order to support those kinds of changes. There were dozens of hours of work that went into that, but also, the collaboration was a big part of the reason that that kind of change was implemented. I really appreciate that kind of work. As much as I love the individual words where we're like, "Yes, let's add that," I also really appreciate the bigger structural changes because I think that in those cases, we're able to show how dynamic a vocabulary like ours can be and how much we can adapt to use cases and to community need.

Belantara: A little earlier in the interview you talked about the kind of joy that the board felt going in and removing a bunch of terms that seemed like you could remove them from what this new idea of what the *Homosaurus* should focus on. Could you tell us some of the terms that you removed during that time?

Rawson: A lot of them were not terribly interesting. A lot of them were just the broader terms that were the broadest terms in the vocabulary: things like arts, literature, and performance, the really top-level terms. Some of the other terms that we took out with a more political bent were things related to pedophilia, for example. We looked at that and said, "Why do we have terms for pedophilia in this vocabulary? What is it doing here and how are we perpetuating already inaccurate stereotypes of gay communities by making any kind of relationship to pedophilia visible in this space?"

That was one term that was actually not taken out until much later. There're things like that that sometimes surprise us when they still remain in the vocabulary. We forgot to take them out, or we didn't really think through what the implications of it would be to have certain terms within it. Another term that we've struggled with, and I'm not quite even sure how to talk about it because there's slurs in some of our terminology, is people who are attracted to trans people. How do we account for those folks in the vocabulary? Is there a way of doing so that is not disrespectful to trans people? That's a set of terms that we have often grappled with and that we are still in the process of revising.

Belantara: A little while ago, again, during that same conversation, you mentioned the joy, but you've also written about the process of revision as joyful and cathartic. Can you tell us more about the feelings generated in your stages of revision?

Rawson: One of my favorite earlier memories of the project, before everyone started working from home, is that we would have several of our board members who were in cubicle settings who would try to talk about these terms and they felt like they couldn't say the words out loud. You'd hear someone whispering, "butt plug," or something like that. Or when it was too racy, they would actually just call out the column and row number on a spreadsheet.

It was this beautifully charming moment where we were all in on it together. We were talking about something that we knew the straight world around us was not in on and we would just laugh and giggle, and, you know, some of the terms that we have in the vocabulary are just funny, especially when you say them aloud in a group of queer and trans folks who don't get to talk about these things aloud very often. It's just been a really fun process. I also think that some of us have appreciated what we talk about as the world-building opportunities with the *Homosaurus*.

For a lot of our terms that have an LGBTQ+ prefix, we then build out those terms as having narrower terms under that. For example, this is the one we talk about all the time: we have *LGBTQ+ beaches*, and then under that we have *Gay beaches* and *Lesbian beaches*, and both of those are a thing, but *Bisexual beaches*, at least to my knowledge, is not really a thing, but it's in the *Homosaurus*. And so, we joke about the bisexual beaches problem because it's one of those instances where we don't know that there's any literary warrant for it, but that's never been the reason why we have terms in our vocabulary. In some cases, we don't say, "We have to see sufficient usage before we will include a term."

We will say, "Yep, that term may not be a thing, but maybe it will be one day."

Of course, invariably, we'll then say, "Oh, we just need a transgender beach and maybe our next *Homosaurus* board meeting should be at a beach and then we can just start calling that the transgender beach."

We joke around about the ways that we might actually use the vocabulary to advance queer and trans community building, not just retroactively describe it.

Belantara: Following along the same train of thought, traditional library cataloging uses literary warrant as a basis for including new terms. Can you talk about the ways queer world making, as you've described it, shapes the *Homosaurus* vocabulary?

Rawson: As we've seen with other vocabularies, literary warrant can be a mechanism of power that excludes queer and trans people, information, and communities, and really limits the visibility that we can have in information contexts. For us, literary warrant was never the basis for the vocabulary, because who gets to make that decision? What are the politics involved? What counts as a literary source? And how do you decide how many need to be included?

It just seems like there are so many opportunities in that process for it to be rife with privilege and decisions about term impacts and significance. I say all that, but at the same time, I will confess that we have had people who have suggested terms to us that we have decided shouldn't be in the vocabulary because they're not used widely enough. Sometimes it might be that a person will just email and say, "Oh, my friends and I have been starting to use this term for ourselves."

And we'll say, "Yes, that's awesome, that's great, but the *Homosaurus* isn't necessarily the place to make a new term more popularized."

This is what's really interesting about this project: I don't know that there's any definitive answer on whether what the project is meant to do is what the project is doing. It may be doing things that we're not aware of yet. It may be opening up linguistic possibilities that we haven't forecasted and maybe that's a great thing. But it also leads me back to this moment where, just as I am critical of those who have kept queer and trans terms out of broader vocabularies, I see that now I'm in the position of doing that with the *Homosaurus*, and so are all of our board members. We are sitting in those positions of power to decide which terms should be in and which terms should be out. It's complicated and it's sometimes problematic, and that's just part of the water we're swimming in with it.

Belantara: What role does hierarchy play in the *Homosaurus*? How has the editorial board approached those aspects of the vocabulary?

Rawson: As a rhetoric scholar, this is one of my favorite things to think about and talk about in the vocabulary. In particular, given my interest in trans studies and trans history, you can see how messy this gets really quickly. For example, a term like *Transsexual*: is that under the *Transgender* umbrella or is it separate from the *Transgender* umbrella? Humanities scholars are often able to dodge these kinds of questions and we use all kinds of qualifiers and verbal gymnastics to be able to preserve the complexity of language. But in a thesaurus, you actually have to put these terms in relation to each other.

There are hierarchies of terms that people would certainly object to, that people would think are problematic or think are a limiting reading of a term, and so forth. In many cases, I would absolutely agree with them. But the thing I appreciate about it is that you're also putting terms in dynamic relationship to each other. For example, if we look at slurs, you can really see what it does to bring together these slurs that often cut across time and context and bring them together side by side in a hierarchical relationship to each other, because it shows you the ways that language has been used for harmful effects.

These hierarchies can often bring together groupings that are not brought together in other ways. What that then does is it really coheres this language around the theme of LGBTQ+ topics, and that is always our ontological orientation; that is where we come back to, and that then allows us to refract all of that terminology through that lens. When else is that happening? That's why I've taken so much joy and pride in this project, because I see all of this opportunity for queer worldmaking through building this vocabulary, and queer communities have done this throughout time. But, to see it in this direct way in an information context I just think is so powerful.

Figure 9. A logo for the *Homosaurus*, created by Cricket Press.

Belantara: As you've mentioned before, the *Homosaurus* is hosted online now in its own space separate from the DTA. I just have a quick question, actually, about the homepage. Who actually designed the homepage, the logo, the rainbow with the Brontosaurus? Could you talk a little bit about what went into making that first page people see and who was behind it?

Rawson: That logo, and we do call it a logo, was designed by these two great artists out of Kentucky. They have a shop called Cricket Press.[7] I'm a big fan of their art. It's the same artist who created the Digital Trans Archive logo and some of our artwork, so you can see some resonance there. But essentially, we had the name *Homosaurus* and we already kind of knew we were headed towards a dinosaur theme. It was really funny because we got a number of different mock-ups for it, and this was actually a moment where there was a little bit of disagreement on the board where you could just sort of see eyebrows raised and people wondering, do we want to go this whimsical? Is this really the tone we're trying to strike, with rainbow dinosaurs?

---

7. Brian Turner and Sara Turner are artists located in Lexington, Kentucky. Their work is available here: https://www.cricket-press.com/.

One of the early designs had a Stegosaurus with rainbow things on its back—you can kind of imagine that one—which was also quite cute. Maybe we'll give the Brontosaurus a companion one day. But since then, it's been one of the touchstones of the project. People really love the logo and we have a Threadless shop, and I'm always surprised by how much traffic it gets and how much people are buying on the Threadless shop.[8] We actually take any proceeds from that and put them right into our collaborations. But people just love the logo.

That's also been a really successful part of the project: having a visualization to go along with it. I will say, too, candidly, that I think our website really has been a bit neglected in terms of its visual appeal because so much of our focus is on the vocabulary, and we really haven't put a lot of energy and effort into a splashy website. It just has not been our priority. If you go to visit the website, it will be a very straightforward and functional site, but I think it does its job right now and on the docket in the next few years will definitely be a bit of a makeover. But the logo is not going anywhere.

Belantara: Yeah, don't let that logo go. It's beautiful. And so, you've described the *Homosaurus* as a linked data vocabulary hosted online. What does it mean that the vocabulary is linked data and how is that different from a print thesaurus?

Rawson: Often, people think a linked data vocabulary is just a digital or online version of a printed thesaurus, for example. And it's not, it's a bit different than that. This is actually something that is really helpful for us and for our future growth as well. A linked data vocabulary, in its essence, provides each concept with a URI—and I'm trying to try not to get to too techy here—a Uniform Resource Indicator, so that anyone can access that term through the URI.

Even if the term were to change slightly or something were to shift a bit, the URI would remain stable. That's a really helpful thing for in-

---

8. The Threadless shop is accessible here: https://homosaurus.threadless.com/designs/homosaurus-logo.

formation contexts because it means that the vocabulary can be pretty dynamic, whereas the URIs remain stable and those URIs then can connect to other information environments. It allows linking across different databases and other sites that are linking back to that same concept. Now, again, this is me being really theoretical and getting excited as a rhetoric scholar, but one thing that's helpful to remember in a linked data vocabulary is that the URI is separate from the expression of that concept.

So, you can have the concept at the URI level and then you can have the expression of that in a particular term. In our case almost all of our terms are in English, but as we're looking ahead and thinking about translations into other languages, that space gives us a tremendous opportunity to not only map terms into multiple languages that can share a singular URI and then just be expressed in different languages, but it also allows us to make sure that English is not the basis for which all other terms are then translated from.

We can create this multi-language LGBTQ+ thesaurus that is really meant to be dynamic and non-hierarchical in the sense of its language expressions. And to me, that is such a powerful way of being able to connect resources globally. I've given you a bit of a preview of where we're thinking about going in the next few years, but linked data will allow us to do that pathbreaking work.

Belantara: And as linked data online vocabulary, the *Homosaurus* is free to be used by anyone on the open web who uses the vocabulary. Have there been any uses that have surprised or dismayed you?

Rawson: One of the interesting things is we're not always aware of who's using it. Because we have lots of different formats where you can download the vocabulary, people will download it and then use it through their own local databases or in catalogs, and we're not necessarily aware of how they're using it or the terms that they're implementing. We do hear about it from users when they have trouble, when they have recommendations for new terms, and when they're really excited about it and want to shout about it from the rooftops.

We recently started a user community and it's just a simple Google group[9] where we are able to bring people together and they can email and post to each other. From what we've seen from that group, we have predominantly U.S. and Canadian users, lots of institutions of higher ed, a lot of public libraries, and we've also seen some museum and archives usage. Because I'm not in the library world, I didn't realize how many library vendors would want to use it. That has been interesting for the board to figure out where we might have lines around that.

For example, if a for-profit company approaches us and wants to use our logo, especially in June when they are talking about implementing *Homosaurus* terms in the packages that they're selling to libraries, as a board we have come down on the side of not being super comfortable with for-profit companies making a profit off of our volunteer labor. Because I'm not in the library world, that surprised me. I guess I was kind of naive to all the machinery involved around libraries, and there's certainly a lot of it, and it's far more complicated than I have any awareness of. But that was one use case that was a bit surprising.

I also have been surprised by the number of people who have reached out about it who are not in libraries and archives. I've just sort of wondered, how did you find this and what is your interest in it? And they're just language wonks who are just super excited about queer terminology and who might just reach out and say, "What about this term?"

And I'd respond, "Well, what's your interest in it?"

They'll say, "Well, I just found the vocabulary and I want to contribute." And so, that's also been fun to see.

Belantara: In a 2022 article written by you and Marika,[10] who's also on the board, you mentioned her before, you discussed the tensions between correcting and expanding descriptive language for queer materials and

---

9. The *Homosaurus* user community can be found here: https://groups.google.com/g/homoitcommunity.

10. Cifor, M., & Rawson, K. J., "Mediating Queer and Trans Pasts: The *Homosaurus* as Queer Information Activism," *Information, Communication & Society* 26, no. 11 (2022): 1-18.

the impossibility of ever getting it right. Can you tell us more about that dynamic and how does it shape the work that the board does together?

Rawson: It's funny because we used a lot of Emily's theoretical work[11] to support that article. One of the ways that we've thought about the purpose of the *Homosaurus* is just to provide more terminology, make more words available to be used to enhance discoverability. And sometimes that's just about making things legible and possible so that when a user comes into an information environment and they start doing searches, they can find themselves reflected, and they can find the experiences that they're looking for, the information that they're seeking in that space where it might not have been searchable or discoverable before.

So, on the one hand, part of our job is to just get more terms out there, to have more terms so that there is more opportunity for description. Especially in linked data and digital environments, the proliferation of terminology is incredibly important, to just add more terms, more opportunities, and more points of access to folks. But the other part of it is hearkening back to the worldmaking conversation we were having earlier, which is also thinking about what it means to include the kinds of complexity and relationships and the dynamics that we are trying to capture in the vocabulary.

That hits more of a theoretical register, and I think a few of us on the board are especially inclined to think about the vocabulary in those ways and to think about what we can do with these terms, even if we're anticipating future usage, rather than reflecting on past usages. Because in a cataloging environment, you're in this weird temporality where you're trying to account for things that have already been produced, and you're anticipating future users, but you're describing in the present. Especially with LGBTQ+ terms, where you know that things are going to be out of date ten seconds from now, how do you try to navigate that temporality?

---

11. Drabinski, Emily, "Queering the Catalog: Queer Theory and the Politics of Correction," *Library Quarterly* 83, no. 2 (2013): 94-111.

For me, it's a fun moment. But I will say, as someone who directs a digital archive, that I look back and I'm like, "Oh, that was a bad decision and now I want to go back and do some changes to our earlier metadata."

Who has the time or resources for that kind of work? But that's, I think, precisely what a queer vocabulary does. It really helps us to think about the dynamic nature of language in these spaces and how those of us who are working within these information environments are impacting the language and then impacting not only current and future users, but the ways that those earlier materials are considered and thought of and framed. How are we anticipating and shaping future uses based on how we are describing those materials in the present?

Drabinski: Can you tell us a bit about how you think about *Homosaurus* and its capacity to describe queer identity across culture and time? Is there a way that *Homosaurus* can account for that movement in language that you've been talking about?

Rawson: There's a way that I hope it can account for it, but I don't know that it always does. We've spent a lot of energy investing in our scope notes, for example. And for those of you who aren't super into thesaurus terminology, a scope note is kind of like a definition, except that it's advice on how to implement a term; so, it's distinct from a definition in that it's not trying to set out all of the meaning of a term, but it's trying to guide users on how they should be implementing that term.

The problem is that scope notes, like some of the deeper descriptions that we do in any information environment, sometimes get lost. People see the higher-level term and they just apply that term. One example of that might be the term *Transvestite*, which is a very specific, historical term. It's still used in some contemporary contexts, but it's generally fallen out of favor. The scope note for that term says something to the effect that it should only be used in historical context, but we have certainly seen use cases where that has not been the case, where it has been used as if it is synonymous with, for example, transgender. And those are the moments where I'm thinking, all right, how do we convey this better? How do we help to keep the complexity of the terms at play when sometimes they are attached in a simplified way?

Part of that is because lots of folks who are using the vocabulary are not in queer and trans communities and so they do not have that language available to them. I think it's our job to support those users and to figure out how we can better help inform the terms that they choose and the context in which they apply them. But it is a tremendous challenge, especially as we're thinking about how this is an international vocabulary and that will continue to be created in multiple languages.

Just thinking about all of the, not only historical, but cultural and contextual dynamic forces that are at work for all of these terms…it's mind boggling how to help support nuanced uses and applications of those terms. But there have definitely been a lot of places in which I've seen terms not quite matching up with our scope notes as we've tried to support particular uses of them.

Drabinski: You described in this article that we've referenced a couple of times, that the *Homosaurus* is a project that is destined to fail. Can you tell us more about how you think about failure in the context of the *Homosaurus*?

Rawson: I appreciate that prompting, especially after that quote because it may sound like such a pessimistic approach to the project. But I always say it with a smile on my face because I think of failure in a queer theoretical framing where failure can sometimes be a productive and helpful and important thing, particularly within a broader cultural framework that dictates certain norms of success and normalcy—that queer and trans folks have vested interests in pushing back against and eschewing.

If you imagine the *Homosaurus* as ever getting to a point where we comprehensively and accurately capture LGBTQ+ language practices, we're never going to do that. In that sense we're happy to fail because I think that part of the beauty of queer and trans language is that it's always pushing back against norms and normalcy and standardization, and part of what we're doing with the *Homosaurus*, of course, is codifying queer and trans language practices. Sometimes I think, maybe we shouldn't include that term—to let it be totally counter-cultural for a while. But then I think, wow, you're going to have someone coming into a library and searching for that term and how mind-blowing would it be when they actually can find materials related to that term?

So, we're in this really precarious position of, in some ways, institutionalizing the very language that we love so dearly because it refuses institutionalization, or it refuses to be normed and structured. It's a funny position to be in. So, when the vocabulary fails or when we see parts of it that are kind of messy, I actually appreciate that because I think it speaks to the impossibility of the whole project, and not just the impossibility, but the undesirability of making it perfect, of ever making it static and comprehensive and 100% accurate.

Drabinski: Can you tell us a bit about how you document your own work? Thinking about the *Homosaurus* and its history, how are your board documents archived and what do you think is most important to document about the group's work?

Rawson: I'm chuckling because, just like with the DTA, I don't think the *Homosaurus* does a good enough job of documenting ourselves and telling our own story. I appreciate opportunities like this interview because I think this will be a really helpful contribution to that story and the narrative of the work that we're doing. We are dutiful in keeping our notes and keeping proposals and keeping digital history of all of our conversations to the extent that we account for them in our notes. But beyond that, a lot of it comes down to the vocabulary itself and the versioning.

What we're trying to roll out in the next few months is more access to earlier versions so you can toggle between different versions of the vocabulary. I think that would be, more than anything else, a really important reflection of our past work. It would be great if we rolled out some data visualization where you can look at the terms that have come on board and the terms that were deleted over time. There are these lovely little research projects that could spin off of the *Homosaurus* and that's certainly one of them. But I think that on the whole, we have not been focused on documenting the work that we're doing because we're so focused on the work that we're doing.

I think that is a common experience for most oppressed groups and organizations representing oppressed people, is that we are often just in it. You know, we have our sleeves rolled up and we're doing the work and then, at some point, someone looks around and says, "Oh yeah, shouldn't we be keeping better track of this?" So, I appreciate this reminder that we might attend more to that for the future as well.

It was just this beautifully charming moment where we were all in on it together. We were talking about something that we knew the straight world around us was not in on and we would just laugh and giggle. Some of the terms that we have in the vocabulary are just funny, especially when you say them aloud in a group of queer and trans folks who don't get to talk about these things aloud very often.

Belantara: Just want to ask a quick follow up question. When you mention that you're keeping notes and your minutes and things, what do you use to store those and where are they accessible?

Rawson: Right now, they're all Google Docs and in Google Sheets and things in the Google-verse. We could have a longer conversation about the benefits and limitations of that. I also keep backup copies of things, so I have things saved. But right now, we use the Google-verse to facilitate collaborations.

Drabinski: Speaking of collaborations, how do you sustain the collaborative nature of the editorial board and do you have any succession plans in place?

Rawson: I think that the best way that we have maintained our collaborative nature is continuing to enjoy one another. Honestly, mutual respect and interdependence, for us, has always come back to queer joy, to enjoying being around each other, caring where each other is at right now, and what's happening in our lives. For us, that has really sustained the energy behind the project. It has certainly also helped to see how widely it's being used and how much energy and excitement there is for it. And I think we're just at the beginning of seeing the uptake for the project. I think that it's about to explode even more than it already has, which is kind of an exciting place to be in.

We don't have any succession plans right now, aside from the fact that we have a lot of board members with a lot of energy. So, there's just a ton of goodwill and enthusiasm behind the project. We just talked about our board structure a few days ago, and in that conversation we discussed, do we even need a Chair? Why do we need a leadership structure? Maybe we can have a really queer organizational structure? And then we decided that for grants and other things there needs to be some sort of legibility, which is how I ended up still with the title of Chair.

But as a group, there's just so much commitment to this work that thus far, we have not really had to be overly concerned with what happens if all the board members fade out. We've had the opposite problem of having too many people who want to join the board, and we are not able to bring many new folks on because no one wants to leave. We also talked about whether there should there be term limits, but everyone responded, "But this work is so much fun." So, we decided to find other opportunities for folks to collaborate, and we're really thinking about working group structures and other ways that we can create formal opportunities for other people to get more deeply involved in the project.

Drabinski: Can you tell us what's next for the *Homosaurus*? What do you see as the most important next directions?

Rawson: I'm hoping that we are able to secure some funding for creating the *Homosaurus* in other languages. I always have to hold myself back from saying "translations," because I think that's the wrong approach to think about it. We really want to build the administrative environment that will allow for other versions of the *Homosaurus* to be built and then mapped across to English, but obviously, not in all term cases.

What that looks like and how we bring together collaborators is a big next step for us. Folks who are working on translations into several different languages—sorry, I've called it translations, in part because some of our collaborators call it that because I think they start with the English version and go from there—but we also want to figure out how to support the development of LGBTQ+ terms in other language contexts and cultural contexts that are not mappable to English. We want to think about how do we create those conversations? How do we support these working groups? And it's a really interesting set of organizational questions, especially when you get to language considerations when not everyone speaks English.

How do you communicate and how do you really connect with folks and how do we continue to have that joy that we've been able to build on the editorial board and bring that into other spaces related to the *Homosaurus*? I think that's where our attention might go in the next few years.

Belantara: Just a quick follow up about incorporating terms that do not have the same terminology in English. In those situations, will you be adding the scope notes in that language? And then where, in fact, or how will the translation take place for people who might be wanting to incorporate that term with English language materials?

Rawson: When we first started scoping out this work, we didn't even think about all of the other fields, like scope notes and history notes, and I think that just shows you how easy it is to get tunnel vision or even just think on the theoretical level rather than the practical level on a project like this. The short answer is, of course, we have to have everything available in whatever language the vocabulary is being built in, but then the mappings also need to be in multiple languages.

We're trying to upend the logic of having an English-based project and, instead, think about what it might mean to create a different kind of multilingual digital environment. Because we are in a moment where that is very doable; it's just the limitations of our own thinking, rather than any technological limitations.

Drabinski: Do you think the *Homosaurus* will ever be done?

Rawson: Never. And in fact, it's funny you asked that because some of the terms we worked on as a board very closely several years ago have already surfaced as some terms that need more attention. There are things that I remember spending multiple meetings on and now we're like, "Oh, that needs some more work."

I think, even if we don't travel too far down the road of multi-language *Homosaurus*-es, we have a lot of work to continue doing with the English-based version. There are so many more terms that we can add and refine and the relationships that we can build among terms, so I don't think our work will ever be done.

Belantara: What would be some of your advice for anybody else who might be wanting to undertake a similar project?

Rawson: A number of different projects have reached out to say, "How can we create something like the *Homosaurus*?"

There's the software answer, where we share our platform and the backend and the development work that we've done. We post things on GitHub, so we try to be as open and accessible as possible. But then there are also more of the organizational and leadership questions, and for me, that's been one of the more interesting parts of the project. How do you create a resource that's based around a community and get sufficient community input beyond the individual people working on a project?

I've had some great conversations with folks who are trying to start vocabularies and are really grappling with that question. And I think it's an ongoing question that we are working on, too, and we can only benefit from more projects like this, continuing to do this kind of work and then collaborating with each other. I've been really excited to hear about other projects that are trying to create their own vocabularies, and then what they're doing with those vocabularies and then how the *Homosaurus* team can learn from what they're up to as well. I've been pleased that there are folks who are reaching out to me about that, and I'm excited to see what they're up to and how we can all support each other's work.

Belantara: And so, Emily and I have come to the end of our interview guide, but now we'd just like to leave some space for you, K.J., to add any closing thoughts or if, perhaps, we should have asked you something and we didn't ask you about it. This is your space to add anything that we might have missed.

Rawson: I can't think of anything offhand that we've missed. I feel like this has been a really great conversation, that it's covered a lot of ground, and also covered a lot of depth at the same time. I feel like this is probably the best opportunity I've had to reflect back and to share more about the board's practices.

I would say, the only thing that's been hard is that I'm the only voice representing a group that is very much a group in all senses of the term. I wish I had been able to tap on the shoulder of several board members throughout this conversation and say, "Oh hey, you'd be best equipped to answer that question." Or, "I'd really love your perspective on this." Because I think that's the only thing that our conversation has failed to capture, just being my voice, speaking on behalf of the board.

Adrian Williams on the Homosaurus

Biography

Adrian Williams has been the Cataloging & Metadata Librarian at the University of Kentucky Libraries since January 2020. They are a member of the *Homosaurus* Editorial Board and the ALA Core Subject Analysis Committee. They were a co-convener of the Trans Metadata Collective and a co-author of that collective's *Metadata Best Practices for Trans and Gender Diverse Resources*[1] and are currently a co-convener for the Queer Metadata Collective, which is working on a broader set of recommendations for the creation and revision of metadata about LGBTQ+ people, histories, and contexts. In their off hours, they're a community organizer fighting for tenant protections and better housing conditions in the beautiful state of Kentucky.

---

1. The Metadata Best Practices for Trans and Gender Diverse Resources are available at https://zenodo.org/record/6687057.

About the Interview

The following transcribed interview of Adrian Williams took place on August 30, 2022, as part of the *Ways of Knowing Oral History Project*. The interview was auto transcribed and then edited by Amanda Belantara and Emily Drabinski. Care was taken to not alter the original transcription's contents. However, the editors have formatted the following to improve readability and provided footnotes for clarity where appropriate. The original transcript and recording can be accessed through the *Ways of Knowing Oral History Project* held at NYU Libraries.[2]

Transcript from the *Ways of Knowing Oral History Project*

Interviewee: Adrian Williams, Member of the *Homosaurus* Editorial Board, Cataloging and Metadata Librarian at the University of Kentucky.
Interviewers: Emily Drabinski & Amanda Belantara
Date: Aug 30, 2022
Location: Virtual Interview; University of Kentucky

Emily Drabinski: Today we're interviewing Adrian Williams, Cataloging and Metadata Librarian at the University of Kentucky. The interview was conducted for the *Ways of Knowing Oral History Project*. The interview took place virtually on August 30th, 2022 and was recorded locally by Justin Hicks at the Louie B. Nunn Center for Oral History at the University of Kentucky in Lexington, Kentucky. The interviewers are Amanda Belantara and Emily Drabinski, based in New York City. Adrian, we'd like to start by hearing a little bit about your background in education.

Adrian Williams: I've worked in academic libraries for most of my adulthood. My first role was at a community college, at an African American archive. I was their archival intern, and my role was signing in graduate students and other visitors and making descriptive metadata, well,

---

2. Williams's recording is available here: https://search.library.nyu.edu/permalink/01NYU_INST/1d6v258/alma990098389940107871.

starting a descriptive metadata project for the undescribed materials that that archive had had, and that was my first role, and that was where I got familiar and began to form a love of cataloging and that sort of aboutness of things.

From there I started my MLIS at Florida State University, and I needed to pay for that MLIS and so, in order to do so, I got a job at their library because they offered tuition reimbursement. That was at the medical library there. I was the technical services assistant, and I was hired to do cataloging, but I really did everything because it was a small library. I did circulation and cataloging; I helped with the e-resource management, I helped with reference, and it was a great place to learn what types of librarianship I would be interested in pursuing in the future because I just got to do everything or got to do the entry level role of everything. And so there I really settled on cataloging, and I moved over to the FSU's main library to be their cataloging associate and just do that full time. From there I came here to the University of Kentucky as their cataloging and metadata librarian, and I've been here since January of 2020.

Drabinski: Can you tell us a little more about your area of professional expertise? You said that you grew to love cataloging and metadata work. Can you tell us more about why you've chosen that as your area of focus?

Williams: I chose cataloging because I guess as a twofold reason of professional interest and personal capabilities. I have a fairly low social battery, and so reference never really worked well for me once it got into reference interviews and consultations and whatnot. I loved helping by email, but those conversations never really worked well for me; whereas, with cataloging, I could just be by myself with the book or the DVD or whatever audio visual resource I was cataloging, and I could look through it and go to Classification Web or Library of Congress's website, see what subject headings worked well for describing this resource and what it was about, and it felt very, not necessarily intuitive, but very natural to be able to just put things in their proper place, or as proper of a place as existed at the time, because, of course, subject headings are ever-evolving, and revisions are always happening—so, putting the subject headings that exist within the moment, matching it to that resource as it exists within the moment.

Drabinski: We wanted to zoom out a little bit and talk about your first encounters with the *Homosaurus*. Can you tell us how you learned about the vocabulary and how you felt when you found it?

Williams: I can't remember exactly when was the first time I learned about it. I remember in 2019, back when I was still staff at FSU, and even before that while being a student at FSU, looking for resources on being LGBTQ, being trans, or being non-binary and not being able to; putting in the words that I knew to look for those into the library catalog, and nothing related to what I had just put in bouncing back to me. It was all just medicalized resources or medical resources or histories and encyclopedias, not really memoirs or studies, or just nothing that I could find that actually helped me find what I was trying to find. And then back in 2019, I remember *Homosaurus* being authorized to be used in MARC records and being really excited to start using it.

I hesitate to say this, but trying to go to my supervisor as a staff member and say like, oh, could we maybe start using this? And that supervisor just not being interested. And then I got here and I had the same talk with my supervisor, and this supervisor was very interested. We worked together on a pilot project around pulling all the books that we have with the LCSH *Non-monogamous relationships*, and seeing if any of those could also have the *Homosaurus* term *Polyamory*. And out of those twenty-three resources, which isn't much, but you know, it's twenty-three of them, about twenty of them had to do with polyamory. And so, we added the *Homosaurus* terms to that. From there we were like, okay, which other subject LCSH could we look at?

Well, *Sexual minorities* is pretty broad, and so let's look at that. Let's see what *Homosaurus* terms we can add to that. And when I say we, it was me mostly, but having institutional buy-in is a huge part of doing this work because it means time not spent doing other things, and so my supervisor was very happy for me to not be doing those other things, to offload me a bit so that I could work on comprehensively adding *Homosaurus* to our catalog. I really appreciate that.

	A	B	C	D	E	F	G	H	I
	Published in 3.5 release	Board Approvals (add initials to indicate a single approval)	Type of Change	Preferred Term (linked if possible)	Other Preferred Terms	Alternative Terms (Use For)	Scope Note	Source(s)	Contributor(s)
2	LB	Full Board	New Term	Masks (Erotic)			Masks worn as a fetish fashion accessory or for sensual or sexual play.		Mel Leverich, Leather Archives & Museum
3	Aw	Full Board	New Term	Pup play		Leatherpups	The act of roleplaying as a canine, sometimes with someone acting as a trainer, handler or pet owner, for fun or erotic enjoyment.		Mel Leverich, Leather Archives & Museum
4	Aw	Full Board	Replace current term	Rubber and latex community [replace Rubber subculture]		Rubber subculture	Communities of people with an interest in rubber or latex materials for fashion and kink.		Mel Leverich, Leather Archives & Museum
5	Aw	Full Board	Replace current term	Rubber and latex fetish [replace Rubber sex]		Rubber and latex sex, Rubbersex, Rubber sex	Eroticization of rubber, latex, and related materials.		Mel Leverich, Leather Archives & Museum
6	Aw	Full Board	New Term	Sex-positive feminism		Sex-positive movement	A broad feminist movement, usually compared against the anti-sex or anti-pornography feminist movement, that supports sexual liberation, sex workers, pornography, and freedom of sexual and gender expression.		Mel Leverich, Leather Archives & Museum
7	Aw	Full Board	New Term	Shoe fetish		Shoe kink	Eroticization of shoes such as high heels and boots.		Mel Leverich, Leather Archives & Museum
8	Aw	Full Board	New Term	Sounding (Sex)			Insertion of rods into the urethra, usually for erotic stimulation.		Mel Leverich, Leather Archives & Museum
9	Aw	Full Board	New Term	Title contests		Leather contests, Leather pageants, Titleholders	An annual event in leather and kink communities where contestants compete for a title. Contestants are judged on qualities including their stage presence, appearance, charisma, and ability to be a leader and activist in the community for the length of their title year.		Mel Leverich, Leather Archives & Museum
10	Aw	Full Board	New Term	Hoods (Erotic)		Bondage hoods	A hood used as a head covering or restraint, for kink, erotic play or fashion.		Mel Leverich, Leather Archives & Museum
11	Aw	Full Board	New Term	Inflation (Erotic)		Inflatables	Inflation of the body, parts of the body, clothing, or inflatable objects with air or other substances for sexual arousal or erotic play.		Mel Leverich, Leather Archives & Museum
12	Aw	Full Board	New Term	Kinky people		Sadomasochists, Fetishists, Kinksters, BDSMers	People who participate in kink and/or power exchange relationships.		Mel Leverich, Leather Archives & Museum

Figure 10. Screenshot of *Homosaurus* term database.

Drabinski: Was it exciting when you found *Homosaurus*? Did you feel like it was liberating?

Williams: I had my doubts, to be honest. In my MLIS I had read about the history of different LGBTQ vocabularies and how they were used in a singular library or a group of libraries, but they'd never found wider usage. While I hoped that *Homosaurus* would have wider usage, I knew the history of those other vocabularies and so I just wasn't sure how it would go. But now a couple of years out from starting that pilot project, I've seen several dozen libraries using *Homosaurus* now, and that number grows every week, every month.

I got an email yesterday afternoon asking me, someone had looked at, had watched one of my *Homosaurus* presentations and had a clarifying question around URIs. And so, oh, okay, another user, we got 'em. We got another one. I would say that at the start, I wasn't necessarily excited. I was optimistic. Now I would say as I look into the future of *Homosaurus*, and the present as well, I'm pretty excited about where it's going and where it is right now, how far it's been able to come with the vocabulary it has, with its structure, and how it's grown and expanded and clarified, and also the increase in users that we've had. I find that pretty exciting.

Drabinski: Were there any terms that interested or excited you when you saw them in the *Homosaurus*?

Williams: A lot of the terms specifically related to different cultures. So, like, the terms *Tom* and *Dee*, which are used in Thai lesbian culture, or the term *Māhū*, which is used in Hawaiian culture—these very culturally specific terms are what excited me the most. Seeing terms that are used by a people without translation, without colonialism sort of twisting, or not twisting, but making it fit into the vocabulary, like, letting it be for its own sake versus trying to make it fit. LCSH, as you know, it needs to be in English, or if it's not in English, there needs to be a parenthesized English term. There needs to be some equivocation there, some reconciliation. With *Homosaurus*, there doesn't need to be any reconciliation there. It can just be. So those culturally specific terms are what excite me the most.

Drabinski: When you initially reviewed the vocabulary, did you see anything that was missing?

Williams: Something that was missing that I'm working on expanding right now as part of the board are the different ethnicity terms. We had African American librarians, we had Latinx librarians, but we didn't have Indian librarians, we didn't have Chinese librarians—not librarians, lesbians! We didn't have Chinese lesbians, we didn't have Indian lesbians, we didn't have Pakistani lesbians. Adding those ethnicity-specific terms has been something that I've been working on. That's one. This isn't something that I noticed but was pointed out to me by Bri [Watson] at the time when I was coming onto the board, we didn't have many terms around asexuality or aromanticism, and many of those terms have been added.[3] I think there are a few more.

Drabinski: I'm interested in how intersectionality works inside of the *Homosaurus*, and the intersections of gender and sexuality terms with terms related to race and ethnicity. I wonder if you could say a bit more about how you see that working in the *Homosaurus* and how the *Homosaurus* has affordances for that that we don't see in traditional cataloging systems.

Williams: With LCSH, you're not going to see—you will see African American gay men. You do see African American women, African American gay men, African American lesbians, but it's not really supposed to be there anymore. It's supposed to be in LCDGT, and so there's this fragmentation of what's allowed versus not allowed in these different LOC vocabularies.

Drabinski: How are race and class and other axes of difference, disability, language of origin, how do those work inside of *Homosaurus*, and do you see a difference between how intersectionality is managed in *Homosaurus* versus how it's dealt with in LOC?

Williams: Obviously *Homosaurus* is an LGBTQ+ vocabulary, so everything that is added to the vocabulary has to be from some sort of queer context. That being said, every group has queer people. Every ethnicity, every class structure has queer people, and so when there is a gap in that structure, when it's noticed, say, that we don't have terms for Two Spirit identity or other Indigenous genders, Indigenous sexualities, something that we've done is to reach out to groups to see what terms they would like added to the vocabulary, how they would like to be described.

---

3. Bri Watson is a member of the Homosaurus board.

That's something that we've done. When we notice that one term is missing, we ask ourselves, well, what other terms are missing around this? How can we not just add this term, but how can we build this out? How can we just add further context to the living history that is queerness, that is transness?

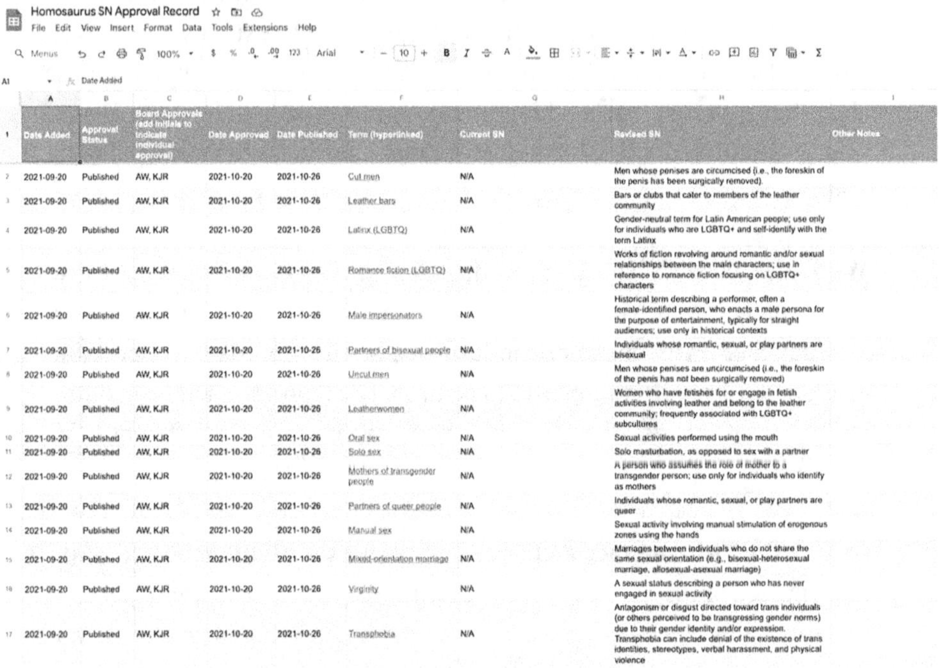

Homosaurus SN Approval Record

	Date Added	Approval Status	Board Approvals (add initials to indicate individual approval)	Date Approved	Date Published	Term (hyperlinked)	Current SN	Revised SN	Other Notes
2	2021-09-20	Published	AW, KJR	2021-10-20	2021-10-26	Cut men	N/A	Men whose penises are circumcised (i.e., the foreskin of the penis has been surgically removed).	
3	2021-09-20	Published	AW, KJR	2021-10-20	2021-10-26	Leather bars	N/A	Bars or clubs that cater to members of the leather community	
4	2021-09-20	Published	AW, KJR	2021-10-20	2021-10-26	Latinx (LGBTQ)	N/A	Gender-neutral term for Latin American people; use only for individuals who are LGBTQ+ and self-identify with the term Latinx	
5	2021-09-20	Published	AW, KJR	2021-10-20	2021-10-26	Romance fiction (LGBTQ)	N/A	Works of fiction revolving around romantic and/or sexual relationships between the main characters; use in reference to romance fiction focusing on LGBTQ+ characters	
6	2021-09-20	Published	AW, KJR	2021-10-20	2021-10-26	Male impersonators	N/A	Historical term describing a performer, often a female-identified person, who enacts a male persona for the purpose of entertainment, typically for straight audiences; use only in historical contexts	
7	2021-09-20	Published	AW, KJR	2021-10-20	2021-10-26	Partners of bisexual people	N/A	Individuals whose romantic, sexual, or play partners are bisexual	
8	2021-09-20	Published	AW, KJR	2021-10-20	2021-10-26	Uncut men	N/A	Men whose penises are uncircumcised (i.e., the foreskin of the penis has not been surgically removed)	
9	2021-09-20	Published	AW, KJR	2021-10-20	2021-10-26	Leatherwomen	N/A	Women who have fetishes for or engage in fetish activities involving leather and belong to the leather community; frequently associated with LGBTQ+ subcultures	
10	2021-09-20	Published	AW, KJR	2021-10-20	2021-10-26	Oral sex	N/A	Sexual activities performed using the mouth	
11	2021-09-20	Published	AW, KJR	2021-10-20	2021-10-26	Solo sex	N/A	Solo masturbation, as opposed to sex with a partner	
12	2021-09-20	Published	AW, KJR	2021-10-20	2021-10-26	Mothers of transgender people	N/A	A person who assumes the role of mother to a transgender person; use only for individuals who identify as mothers	
13	2021-09-20	Published	AW, KJR	2021-10-20	2021-10-26	Partners of queer people	N/A	Individuals whose romantic, sexual, or play partners are queer	
14	2021-09-20	Published	AW, KJR	2021-10-20	2021-10-26	Manual sex	N/A	Sexual activity involving manual stimulation of erogenous zones using the hands	
15	2021-09-20	Published	AW, KJR	2021-10-20	2021-10-26	Mixed-orientation marriage	N/A	Marriages between individuals who do not share the same sexual orientation (e.g., bisexual-heterosexual marriage, allosexual-asexual marriage)	
16	2021-09-20	Published	AW, KJR	2021-10-20	2021-10-26	Virginity	N/A	A sexual status describing a person who has never engaged in sexual activity	
17	2021-09-20	Published	AW, KJR	2021-10-20	2021-10-26	Transphobia	N/A	Antagonism or disgust directed toward trans individuals (or others perceived to be transgressing gender norms) due to their gender identity and/or expression. Transphobia can include denial of the existence of trans identities, stereotypes, verbal harassment, and physical violence	

Figure 11. Screenshot of approved *Homosaurus* terms

Belantara: I just want to ask a follow up question to something you mentioned a moment ago, and apologies if I get the acronym wrong, but you referenced the LCDGT.[4] Did I say it?

Williams: Yeah, demographic group terms.

Belantara: Could you tell us a little bit about what that is exactly?

4. LCDGT refers to the Library of Congress Demographic Group Terms. More information can be found here: https://www.loc.gov/aba/publications/FreeLCDGT/freelcdgt.html.

Williams: Back in around 2012 or so, well after Library of Congress Genre Form Terms were made a thing, genre form terms were meant to be separated out from subject headings so that you could put in the MARC record that this is a children's book, this is a documentary, this is a clarinet performance. That was separated out from Library of Congress Subject Headings and it got people asking, well, if genre/form terms can be separated out, can we also separate out demographic group terms?

I wasn't in these conversations because I was in high school or whatever, and so my recollection and my understanding of this might not be perfect. But can we also separate out demographic group terms because they're not a subject really. If we were to separate out demographic group terms, where would we put them in the record? What would they be used for? And what they're used for right now in 2022 is to tell the reader: What is the audience for that work? And who is the creator of that work? And that's put in the 385 field and the 386 field, if I remember correctly.

With LC Demographic Group Terms, if you have a book that is meant for Catholic students, you can say that this book is meant for Catholic students. If you have several works that were created by Maldivian priests, there is a term that you could use and you can say, oh, these works were all created by Maldivian priests. And if anyone is looking for works created by Maldivian priests then they can just search for it, and it's perfect and awesome. So that is demographic group terms, but it is also, obviously, limited because what is this book for? Who is this book for? Who is this book by? It is not: who is this book about? That's a completely different thing. And so, *Homosaurus* is the subject part of that. You can still use demographic group terms if you have books written by trans men. You can say that these books were written by transgender men, and you can also have the *Homosaurus* term *Transgender men* to say that this book is about transgender men.

Belantara: You've already talked about this a little bit, but I wanted to delve in a bit deeper. You've presented before on your work integrating *Homosaurus* terms into your local catalog at the University of Kentucky.

Can you tell us about how that project got started and why you felt it was so important?

Williams: As I said before, being a student, being a user of libraries, I've been trying to find information and books about myself for a lot of my life, and I couldn't really find those books very easily. Seeing that this vocabulary exists to make it easier to find these books, to discover these works, I felt pretty optimistic about it. I wanted to help the users that I serve better find our LGTBQ+ resources. I know they exist because I catalog them. They pass through my desk. That's how that project got started, just wanting to make it easier for LGBTQ students and younger researchers to find these works in the way that they would think to search by them. A lot of the undergraduate students, they wouldn't type *Sexual minorities--United States*. They would type *LGBTQ people*, *Non-binary people*. Some of them would search *Gender nonconforming people*, but not all of them, and so it's helpful to have both of those terms in the catalog for them to search by both *Gender nonconforming* and *Non-binary* and *Gender diverse*, et cetera.

Yeah, so I started on those projects. I did a presentation at the 2021 LD4 Conference, and when I did that presentation, I would say I was midway through that more comprehensive sexual minorities project, and it was also there that the *Homosaurus* board was giving a presentation as well, and so they attended my talk and I felt very starstruck and nervous, like *K.J. is here, oh my God*. And then from there, K.J. contacted me about possibly joining the board and asked how I would feel about it, the work that I thought I could do. I attended a meeting and it went well. I could see a place for myself and a space for myself in doing that more editorial work, and so I hopped on in.

Belantara: In terms of integrating the *Homosaurus* terms into the library where you work, did you face any institutional resistance to the project?

Williams: No, not at all. I had the support of my supervisor, and I'll be honest, this was 2020 and Breonna Taylor was happening, George Floyd was happening, and a lot of the administration was interested in showing that no, we're a progressive place.[5] We do good social justice work over here. There's just a lot of support around that kind of thing, to be honest. So no, I didn't get any pushback.

Belantara: Did any of your colleagues express any type of concerns in terms of being able to implement the new terms?

Williams: They didn't, but I also didn't tell the reference librarians about it until things were already underway, and they were excited because at least a couple of them had interactions with students where they had to apologize for the terms that they were typing in to describe how they were searching for trans people and LGBTQ people, and so they appreciated that they wouldn't necessarily have to type in just those terms anymore.

Drabinski: You mentioned the uprisings that were happening around the time that you got approval to get this project underway. Did that external political ferment shape anything about the urgency of the work for you? Do you feel like your work in the library is influenced by those external political contexts?

Williams: I would say around that time and for a lot of that year, and even still, especially when I'm outside biking and just sort of existing in the outside world, I feel pretty helpless. As a Black person, if I am biking too fast and someone takes it the wrong way or someone is concerned that I might be like, *hmm*.

Ahmaud Arbery really made me very scared for myself because all he was doing was taking a jog and he had his earphones in, and that's me for a lot of the time I'm outside.[6] I'm on my bike with my earphones

---

5. Breonna Taylor was murdered by police officer Myles Cosgrove on March 13, 2020 in Louisville, Kentucky. George Floyd was murdered by police officer Derek Chauvin on May 25, 2020 in Minneapolis, Minnesota. Their deaths sparked one of the largest protest movements in U.S. history as millions of people joined the struggle against police brutality against Black Americans.

6. Ahmaud Arbery was murdered on February 23, 2020, by three white men, Travis McMichael, Gregory McMichael, and William Bryan, in a racially-motivated attack. Arbery had been running in his neighborhood in Glynn County, Georgia

in, just living my life, and to know that I could just be living my life and someone takes that the wrong way and punishes me for it, it just makes me feel very scared and helpless. Working on this project, it made me feel to a certain extent that I was at least doing something for someone. It made me feel that at least I was doing something. I felt less helpless, even though it doesn't make a difference with how my race is treated by others. It could make someone slightly less ignorant to find a resource and maybe even read it, or maybe even watch that documentary.

Belantara: When you're working on this project, do you collaborate with others at the library? And if so, how do you work together?

Williams: I don't really because I'm the primary cataloger. There's the cataloger for oral histories. I talked with her a couple times about how she could use *Homosaurus*, and so she's used it for LGBTQ interviews that the Nunn Center has done. A lot of my collaborative work has either been on the board itself or with librarians at different libraries who are starting in on this work, and so linking them to different resources, different presentations outside of my presentations, such as if they're at a consortium, linking them to Rachel Fischer's presentation because she implemented *Homosaurus* at a public library consortium.[7]

University of Kentucky is an isolated library. They're not a part of a consortium. The way that we put *Homosaurus* in records, we don't really have to be concerned with it affecting other people's catalogs. But when you're in a consortium, your catalogs are all linked up to each other, and so I link them to those presentations. I give them the documentation that I've written up and answer any questions that they have. That's mostly how I collaborate around this.

Belantara: When you're working on this, how do you choose which records to update, and what are your selection priorities when making decisions around metadata?

---

7. Fischer, Rachel K., "Using the *Homosaurus* in a Public Library Consortium: A Case Study," *Library Resources & Technical Services* 67, no. 1 (2023), https://journals.ala.org/index.php/lrts/article/view/7985/11110.

Williams: Throughout 2020 and 2021, it was all retrospective—just the materials that we had so far on LGBTQ topics and just trying to get all of them enhanced. But these days, now that they've all been enhanced, it is incoming resources. I do the streaming video documentaries. I like for the documentaries to have updated and comprehensive metadata. A lot of them have very general subject headings, like *Gender studies* and *Women's studies*, and that makes me angry to see extremely broad subject headings. Those are the ones that tend to get my attention the most. But also recently published titles that have that current terminology, not just in what I add to them, but in the content matter itself—just making sure that the subject headings match what is actually being talked about in the book.

Adding Homosaurus *to these records improves search, and that makes them more widely searchable. It adds more context around that work and more terms that a user might search by. It works toward accounting for each user's familiarity with that subject and what terms they would use. For the most part, I'm not taking out any LCSH. I am merely adding* Homosaurus.... *I'm only adding another way for people to search for this work.*

Belantara: The *Homosaurus* is a linked data vocabulary hosted online. What does it mean that the vocabulary is linked data, and how is that different from a print thesaurus?

Williams: You have reached my weakness and understanding of this sort of thing. As I understand it, linked data exists within the Semantic Web and it uses URIs to—I understand the description part of things more than I understand the technology part of this. Linked data is meant to be this thing where, eventually, when catalogs can be searched for on Google and on the wider web, you can put in search terms or author names and find them in a library that's close to you. *Homosaurus* is a linked data vocabulary in that the structure of it makes it easier to be integrated into the wider web.

Belantara: What are the affordances and limitations of working with linked open data in a library setting, and why do you think it's important that the vocabulary is built in this way?

Williams: I would say one thing to look out for is that when something exists within a linked open data context, it's freer and looser than an authorized subject heading that is changed and controlled more bureaucratically. There's also that question of *where is this?* I would say that it's easier for a resource to leave the axis of control.

With a book that just exists in a library outside of the Internet, it can just sit on its shelf and be discovered on that shelf and also within the catalog, whereas if a resource exists within a linked open data context, it can be found by anyone, and to a certain extent changed more easily. The metadata around it can be perhaps changed more easily than an isolated resource might be. But that's just my understanding of that. It's not necessarily correct.

Drabinski: Would you be able to integrate *Homosaurus* terms in the local catalog as easily if they weren't adopted as part of the Library of Congress accepted MARC vocabularies? Does that play a role?

Williams: It does play a role in smaller libraries that don't have the time to integrate *Homosaurus* into their catalog by themselves or don't have the resources to do so. They can go to OCLC or WorldShare Record Manager and get the records that have *Homosaurus* already added to them.[8] Having more libraries use *Homosaurus* makes it easier for libraries that just can't integrate it to still get those records, to still get that biblio-

---

8. OCLC's WorldCat and WorldShare Record Manager are cooperative cataloging tools that enable libraries to share catalog records, including those enhanced by additional subject vocabularies like *Homosaurus*.

graphic description. If you're only integrating it locally, that means that only your library can benefit from it, whereas if you're putting *Homosaurus* terms in OCLC or WorldShare Record Manager, multiple libraries can benefit from it.

Belantara: Let's say I'm a cataloger at one of the institutions that you just described that doesn't have the ability to create records using *Homosaurus* and I wanted to search for one that did use it. Is there a way to actually search specifically for records that use it, or is it more a matter of going through all of the results for that particular item and seeing which ones have the abbreviation for *Homosaurus* in the record?

Williams: When a *Homosaurus* term is put into an OCLC record or a WorldShare Record or in your local record, you also put the source code "homoit" beside that term, and then you also put the URI after the source code. You can search by source code to see a record with that title that has that source code in it.

Belantara: That's cool, thank you. I didn't know about that.

Williams: It is cool. That was really how *Homosaurus* was able to get wider usage, is MARC adding a source code for it so that it could be authorized and used well and consistently.

Belantara: Can you tell us about how enhancing records with *Homosaurus* vocabulary has improved access to materials?

Williams: For example, the pilot project that we did with non-monogamous relationships/polyamory, the twenty books that were about polyamory, most of them were also in Spanish, and so they didn't necessarily have the word, and my accent is terrible, but poliamorosa, poliamor, but not polyamory. When you did a subject search for *Polyamory*, none of those texts showed up. But now when you do a subject search for it, all those books show up.

Adding *Homosaurus* to these records improves search, and that makes them more widely searchable. It adds more context around that work and more terms that a user might search by. It works toward accounting for each user's familiarity with that subject and what terms they would use. For the most part, I'm not taking out any LCSH. I am merely adding *Homosaurus*. When a work isn't actually about what the LCSH term that's on it is about, then, yeah, I'll take out the LCSH as per PCC policy, but I'm not taking anything away. I'm only adding another way for people to search for this work.

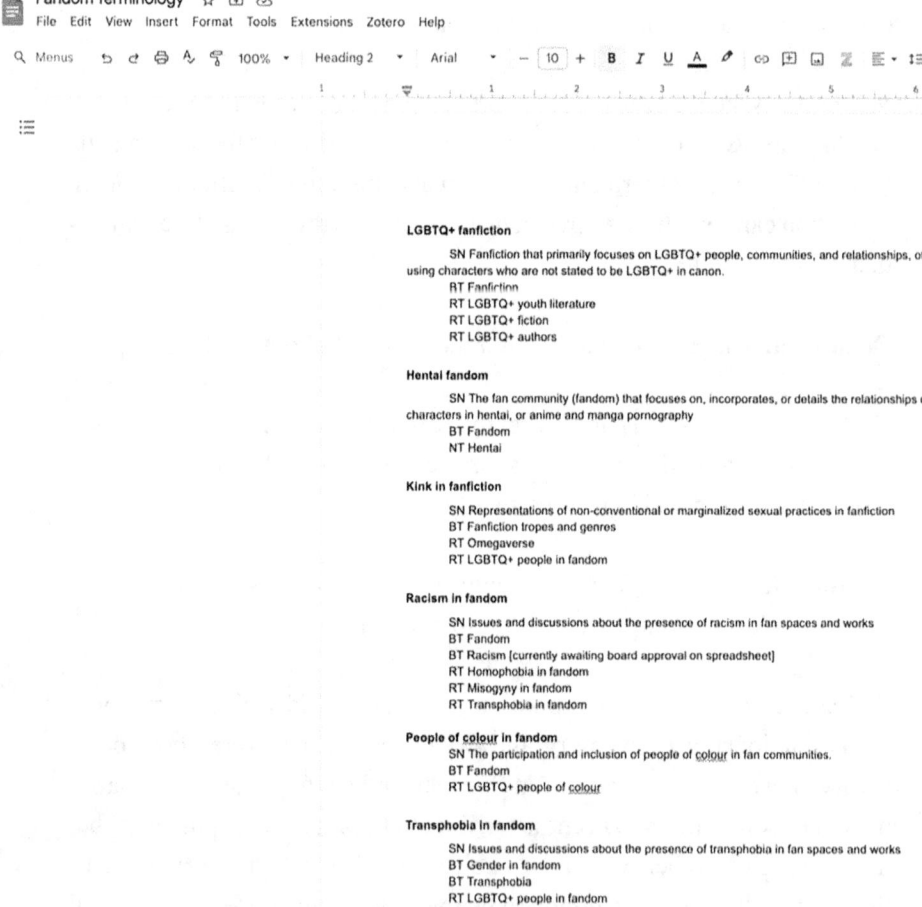

Figure 12. Screenshot showing the relationship of fandom terms in *Homosaurus*.

Belantara: Can you talk about your philosophy behind that decision?

Williams: At an academic library, our primary audience is undergraduate students and graduate students and also faculty—mostly faculty and graduate students when it comes to the library and what is being asked for. But those are not the only people who are going to be searching for things. Also, within those groups there's a diversity of perspective and life experience, and just familiarity, with LGBTQ topics. Yes, I could take out that LCSH that has that more medicalized perspective and that more conservative perspective, but that would also mean that older faculty and older researchers and people just less familiar with current LGBTQ terminology would have more trouble finding it. Keeping the LCSH and adding the *Homosaurus* makes it so that more people can find what we have.

Belantara: Have you gotten feedback on your work in terms of implementing *Homosaurus*? Have you gotten any feedback from people who use the library?

Williams: Well, not from people who use the library because most people who use the library don't know that I, as a cataloger, exist. But I have gotten feedback from the reference librarians here, who are thankful that it exists, that they don't have to just use the more conservative LCSH vocabulary to guide their reference interviews and their consultations around. They can use that more current terminology that the undergraduate students and the graduate students would know. They've been really excited about it.

Belantara: How do you sustain this work inside of your institution, specifically since it sounds like you're the sole person taking this on? How do you manage to prioritize it amongst everything else that you do?

Williams: It's a lot of time blocking, a lot of time management, making sure that I'm working on it consistently. It's hard because it's honestly a lot of work to do. I would say I have the support of my supervisor and offloading at least a couple things that either she can do or one of the staff catalogers can do. Having my supervisor's support and my administration's support has been extremely helpful. Also, I did a lot of this work while we were all at home during quarantine and there weren't physical books that I had to keep track of. I really got a good chunk of this done during quarantine, and I'm really thankful for that.

Now that we are on hybrid schedules, I do a lot of this work when I'm at home. I have my Alma report of resources that I still need to add terms to, and I work through it on my at-home days for an hour or on my Friday. That's just what I do. In that way I am just consistently chunking away at it. A lot of time management, institutional buy-in, if we're going to use a buzzword here, and self-motivation and passion around it. If I weren't passionate about it, it could have fallen off. It could have fallen by the wayside. But I care a lot about making sure that, one, *Homosaurus* is integrated into our catalog to as much an extent as I can make it, and two, that *Homosaurus* as a vocabulary is well structured and is working well for our users.

Belantara: I have a little follow up question to what you just said. Have you heard about other cataloging librarians or people doing cataloging work? Have you heard of other people also making use of the extra time afforded through the pandemic or remote work? Has that enabled a lot more of this type of work, whether it's with *Homosaurus* or another alternative vocabulary? Have you heard that that's maybe had some positive impact?

Williams: Oh, for sure. Working from home is so great, and that's something that I've heard echoed from a couple of other cataloging librarians. I would say most of the emails I got happened within that 2020, 2021 timescape, but, of course, I still get emails every couple of months or so. I can't speak to too many cataloging librarians and what work they've been able to get done during the pandemic, and, of course, state-to-state, region-to-region, a library's acknowledgement of the pandemic varies so much. I honestly can't really speak for too many catalogers who have been able to integrate this and how the pandemic has helped or hindered that, but from the couple that I've spoken to about it, it's been helpful to just have that time away from the library to do these sorts of retrospective projects and to make these back-burner projects put on the front burner a bit.

Drabinski: We'd like to shift now and talk in a little bit more depth and detail about your work as part of the *Homosaurus* Editorial Board. Can you tell us a bit about how you first got involved with *Homosaurus* and who invited you to that board?

I think of Homosaurus *in the same way that you think of a living document. It's going to change. You can make a change one month and then have to make it again the next month. As I embrace that, I embrace that the changes that we make to the vocabulary are not permanent. They might not even be longstanding, but each change we make is for currency, it's for intuitiveness, it's for the living people that are using this and searching using it.*

Williams: I did a presentation at the LD4 Conference, I believe, in 2020.[9] Linked Data for Libraries is an annual conference that takes place in July and covers topics around linked data, libraries using it, Wikidata, the Semantic Web, stuff like that. *Homosaurus* being a linked data open vocabulary, I sent a proposal in for that conference. So, I presented there. A few members of the editorial board were also there doing a presentation. It was virtual, but they were there. We attended each other's presentations.

They had a discussion about bringing me on as a fellow board member, and I met with K.J. two months after that through Zoom to talk about

---

9. LD4 Community brings library and archives workers together to develop and implement linked open data projects. More information can be found here: https://sites.google.com/stanford.edu/ld4-community-site.

what work I could do on the board and what my interests were, to talk about the board itself and its structure and its history, and why they were bringing me on. I attended the August board meeting as a visitor to just see how things were run and then, in September, I joined.

Drabinski: How did you make the decision to join? Did you have any hesitations?

Williams: I did have hesitations. It's an international controlled vocabulary, but at that time it seemed that it was used mostly in western countries, so, like, the United States, Canada, the Netherlands. I knew that there was one other person of color on the board, but mostly it was white people. I knew that there was interest in being a part of the board by other catalogers, and so I worried about being a token being brought on as another POC, person of color. And so part of my conversation with K.J. [Rawson], the co-chair of the board, was just discussing that there's that thing of, yes, I am Black, and that helps my case because they did not necessarily want to add another white person because they had plenty of white people already.

The difference was between being approached to add representation and another perspective but to also have agency on that board and to have my own say rather than being tokenized, if that makes sense. I wasn't being brought on as a token, I was being brought on to add another perspective and to add another voice to the ongoing conversation, which was how this vocabulary would be developed and expanded and how it would evolve into the future.

Drabinski: What work have you focused on in your time on the board?

Williams: Mostly I've focused on adding those ethnicity and nationality-based terms. I've also just been doing a lot of learning about the history of the board and its structure. I've done a lot of term-based, term creation revision, structure conversations, though a good many of us do those as well. Mostly around ethnicity and nationality, but also just the occasional term here and there, noticing that something is missing, calling it to the attention of the board and then everyone working together to either build out that gap or to talk out a broader change that might need to happen with the vocabulary itself.

Drabinski: Can you tell us a little bit about what the meetings are like? How does the editorial board work together, and if you have any disagreements, how do you resolve them?

Williams: I would say it's a breath of fresh air. I work in an academic library, of course, and academia is very steeped in whiteness and adhering to a certain way of speaking, way of agreement, way of decision making. You have a committee, and that committee has a chair, and that chair has the final decision-making power and all that deferment and politicizing.

I find the editorial board a breath of fresh air separate from those types of academic meetings. A lot of us are academics, but it's very casual. We talk about our cats; we talk about concerts that we went to. It is a board, but it's an extremely queer board that does not [only] know that difficult conversations need to happen—it welcomes those difficult conversations. It welcomes the fact that not everyone is going to agree, and so when disagreements happen, we talk through them and contextualize them. I would say that rarely does anyone leave those contentious discussions feeling wrong or disempowered or not listened to at all, because everyone is listened to.

Everyone has a voice and has the space to say something or to puzzle out something that they may not necessarily be able to articulate once they start in. But by the end of the conversation, they've articulated what they needed to and we've listened and we've talked through the consequences and the different ways that something could go. That is in contrast, I would say, to an academic meeting where things need to take place within that hour and decided, if not within that hour, then by email pretty quickly so that things can keep moving and keep up a pace within the academic cycle. The *Homosaurus* board can sort of sit on something for a few months while things are puzzled out and researched and talked over and everything is, to the best of our ability, considered.

Drabinski: Are they fun?[10]

Williams: They are fun. I'm an extremely anxious person, and so the first couple were mostly nerve-racking because it was so much talking and so much active listening and contextualizing and things that I just didn't know that I needed. I would leave each meeting and I'd be like, okay, I've got to get these three books from the library because I don't know shit about these older historical things. But now I find that, a year in, I'm hitting my stride somewhat and helping out more. Yeah, they're definitely fun. I never leave one thinking, like, oh, that was a snoozefest, because it's not. Everything that we're talking about is interesting.

Drabinski: Traditional library cataloging uses literary warrant as a basis for including new terms. Can you talk about the ways *Homosaurus* develops terms in the absence of literary warrant?

Williams: I would say that it's less in the absence of literary warrant and more like adding in user warrant. If a term is used in a few books, yeah, we know that we need to add it, but also, if it's being used on Twitter or on Tumblr or in other online or in-person spaces, then we add it as well; and so, that's user warrant. We got an email earlier this year from a person asking us to add a term that their friends had made, and it was, like, oh, awesome, cool, good for you. But we've searched around, we've asked people, we've looked it up, and we can't find it being used anywhere by anyone else and so, we're not going to add it. But if this changes and it does end up being used by more people, then we will.

We use literary warrant, but we also use user warrant. We have a rubric of green, yellow, red. Green is a mainstream term that is obvious to add. Yellow is not so obvious, but there is clear context for it, and we

---

10. "They" is in reference to the meetings of the *Homosaurus* board.

can find at least a couple of online or offline spaces that are using that term. Red is a term we can't really find being used anywhere, or we're not sure if it fits within the scope of the vocabulary, or a significant build-out would be needed for the group of terms being added; and so, we have to have a board discussion on whether we need to add this term or should add this term.

Drabinski: Can you tell us about any new terms that have been introduced during your time on the board that may be particularly meaningful to you?

Williams: We have a spreadsheet for terms, as well as scope notes that we're adding. The presentation that the board did at LD4 back in 2021 was them doing a crowdsource project, adding notes to each term that defines and contextualizes that term.[11] Back in 2021, a lot of *Homosaurus* terms did not have current notes. But here in September, 2022, almost all of our terms have notes now, and I think that's a beautiful thing. We have terms that have obvious LGBTQ context and we also have terms that are not so obvious in their context. For example, we have *Amazons* in the vocabulary. Why would Amazons be in the vocabulary? It's not just a Greek mythology—all female warriors—but it's in the *Homosaurus* because the Amazons were used as a cultural symbol in lesbian communities in the 20th century and early 21st century.

And so, having notes for each term, especially for these more historical terms, helps catalogers choose terms that fit for this work. It decreases the possibility of the wrong term being added by someone who wants to add LGBTQ terms to their works but may not be an expert on LGBTQ culture or history. There are a whole lot of straight catalogers. There are a whole lot of straight cis catalogers, and some of them are allies who want to use *Homosaurus* but might not have that familiarity, that education, and so scope notes help with that.

---

11. Williams, Adrian. "Use of the *Homosaurus* as an Alternative Controlled Vocabulary at the University of Kentucky Libraries" (presentation, 2021 LD4 Conference on Linked Data, July 21, 2021).

On the *Homosaurus* site, there is the releases tab, and that has the different terms that are added each cycle. I remember when I was starting in on that comprehensive project here at UK and I came across about five or six books on Arab LGTBQ+ people, but there wasn't a term for that in *Homosaurus*, and there wasn't a term for Arab LGBTQ people in LCSH either, and I was really itching to add that term. It also made me realize, oh, it's not just Arab people that are missing from *Homosaurus*. It's also Indian people that are missing from *Homosaurus*.

There are a number of different people that are missing, so expanding that out and just adding the terms for these different people, it helps, not just myself with these five books that I'm trying to catalog, but it helps other people who also have those books and different books. So: *Arab LGBTQ people, Arab lesbians, Arab gay men, Arab bisexual people*. Adding those terms was really exciting for me because I had put in a little request for it before I was on the board and I was just patiently waiting for it to be added. And then I was brought onto the board and I could just do it myself, and it was like, ah, power. But not corrupt power or anything.

Drabinski: Have any terms been removed from the vocabulary since you've been on the board?

Williams: Well, we did a pretty big change in that we switched from an LGBT linked data open vocabulary to an LGBTQ+ linked data vocabulary, and that meant switching all of the terms that had LGBT in it to LGBTQ+ in it. That affected a lot of things. We had *Lesbian religious groups* and *Gay theology, Lesbian theology,* et cetera, and we switched those too. There are a couple of lesbian religious groups but not a whole lot of specifically gay theology, lesbian theology, and so we redirected it to *Queer theology* that could cover those groups a bit more broadly. We also added the *term LGBTQ+-affirming religious groups* because there isn't a whole lot of religion that's based around queerness, but there are religions that affirm and support queerness.

We switched from *Bisexual theology* to *Queer theology*. We had a bunch of terms on *Gender fluid people, Non-binary people, Transgender people*, but we needed to add terms on identity, so *Gender fluid identity*, *Non-binary identity*, to provide nuance between this is a book about non-binary people, this is a book about non-binary identity, etc. It's just different.

The *Homosaurus* was not always *Homosaurus*. It was first the IHLIA Gay and Lesbian Vocabulary. In those first couple of iterations of this vocabulary, it also included age-based attractions, so *Ephebophilia*, *Gerontophilia*, *Pedophilia*. We removed those terms because they're not queer, necessarily. There is stigma that exists that hate groups have used to tie them to queerness, but we didn't want that stigma in our vocabulary. We did not want to perpetuate that connection and so we removed those age-based attraction terms. Those are some things that we've removed since I came on board.

Drabinski: How do you think about the tensions between controlled vocabularies, which are fixed and reflect a particular moment in time, and the value of controlled vocabulary for information retrieval? Queer vocabulary has changed so rapidly in communities. How do you think about this in the *Homosaurus*?

Williams: I think of *Homosaurus* in the same way that you think of a living document. It's going to change. You can make a change one month and then have to make it again the next month. As I embrace that, I embrace that the changes that we make to the vocabulary are not permanent. They might not even be longstanding, but each change we make is for currency, it's for intuitiveness, it's for the living people that are using this and searching using it.

With LCSH there's a certain amount of, and this is just my perspective on this, with LCSH there's a certain amount of unneeded respect and sentimentalism for some of the terms that we have in it. There is certainly appreciation and nostalgia for the history of the terms that we have in *Homosaurus*, and we, of course, have historical terms as well, but there's no holding onto something just to hold onto it if it's not inclusive, if it's not accessible to the different users that we have.

Belantara: What do you see as some of the most important next directions for the *Homosaurus*?

Williams: Big broad things that we're doing are translating it into different languages so that libraries all over the world can just use it. We know that there are librarians that have already started on translating it at their own libraries. We know that there's a Québécois translation. We know that there's a French translation. I believe there's a Gujarati translation in the works. We're excited to be working with those libraries and also writing grants to do the work ourselves and having the vocabulary translated into more languages. So, that's a big thing.

We are also working on documentation so that librarians, libraries that want to use it, a best practices document or guidance to help in implementing it, so that's a big thing. Also, just continuing to expand it and continuing to make sure that it is current and usable and accessible, and that just takes constant work and pivoting and learning.

Belantara: How do you plan to continue implementing the *Homosaurus* at Kentucky?

Williams: I'll be continuing this work by doing a periodic analytics report of the LGBTQ books that come into our library and adding *Homosaurus* terms to them in that periodic way; and, also, as I think of different LCSH terms that are outdated but still describe LGBTQ people, then pulling reports for the resources that have those LCSH and seeing if I've already enhanced them, and enhancing them if I haven't, continuing that retrospective work in a more targeted way.

Belantara: Can you tell us about any other libraries that are doing similar work to yours?

Williams: I know that Fresno State is getting started on a *Homosaurus* pilot. I know that FSU, where I used to work, is getting started on a pilot as well. *Homosaurus* has this community Google group where users of

Homosaurus can ask questions or ask for feedback about something or just ask the board things. It's not often used, but when it is used, that puts us in touch with even more people. So, Fresno State, New Hampshire State Library, a bunch of people.

Belantara: Do you think the *Homosaurus* will ever be done?

Williams: No, no. LCSH isn't done and *Homosaurus*? There will always be, for as long as there are queer people in the world, we're always going to be finding new ways to describe ourselves as the culture evolves. As new people come into this world, there are going to be different ways that they describe themselves and different ways that they see themselves in relation to each other in a romantic or sexual or queer context.

I remember when *queerplatonic* started being a term that was used. It didn't exist until it did, and then suddenly there was a word to describe this thing that I'm sure has been felt and experienced in different ways throughout human history. There have been different words for it throughout human history, but now today we have this term queerplatonic, and so we can add it to the vocabulary and just sort of contextualize it.

So no, I don't think *Homosaurus* will ever be done, and I look forward to seeing how it evolves in the next decade and in the next twenty or so years. I hope it continues to evolve and exist and prosper throughout the next several years.

Belantara: Now we just want to give a few moments if there's anything that you would like to share or if you want to let us know anything that we should have asked about and that we missed in our interview questions.

Williams: I would say that, and this is something that I say at the end of every presentation that I do about it as well, but, if you're interested in using it, if you see that your library could use it and should use it, then I highly encourage you to do so. I can tell you that it's going to be probably slow work. It's going to take a while because this is all subject analysis. This isn't a batch process that you're going to do once and then it'll be over. It's going to be work that is sustained throughout years, ideally. As you add new materials to your library, your library changes, and that long, slow work is good work. It's worth it.

Bibliography

Berman, Sanford. *Prejudices and Antipathies: A Tract on LC Subject Heads Concerning People*. Metuchen, NJ: Scarecrow Press, 1971.

Capek, M. E. S. "Women and Words: Lists of Our Language." *NWSA Journal* 2, no. 3 (1990): 476-484.

Capek, M. E. S. *A Women's Thesaurus: An Index of Language Used to Describe and Locate Information By and About Women*. New York: Harper & Row, 1987.

Capek, M. E. S. "Wired Words: Developing an Online Thesaurus and Database for Improving Access to Women's Information Resources." *Women and Language* 10, no. 1 (1986): 54.

Castillo-Speed, L. "The Usefulness of the Chicano Thesaurus for Indexing Chicano Materials." In *Biblio-Politica: Chicano Perspectives on Library Service in the United States*, edited by Francisco García-Ayvens and Richard Chabrán, 169-178. Berkeley, CA: University of California, Chicano Studies Publications Unit, 1984.

Castillo-Speed, L. "The Chicano Database and the CD-ROM Experience." In *CD-ROM in the Library Today and Tomorrow*, edited by M.K. Duggan, 73-77. Boston: G.K. Hall & Co, 1990.

Chabrán, R. "Latino Reference Arrives." *American Libraries* 18, no. 5 (1987): 384-388.

Cifor, M., & Rawson, K. J. "Mediating Queer and Trans Pasts: The Homosaurus as Queer Information Activism." *Information, Communication & Society* 26, no. 11 (2022): 2168–85

García-Ayvens, Francisco, and Richard Chabrán, editors. *Biblio-Politica: Chicano Perspectives on Library Service in the United States*. Berkeley, CA: University of California, Chicano Studies Library Publications Unit, 1984.

Gross, Tina, Arlene G. Taylor, and Daniel N. Joudrey. "Still a Lot to Lose: The Role of Controlled Vocabulary in Keyword Searching." *Cataloging & Classification Quarterly* 53, no. 1 (2015): 1-39. DOI: 10.1080/01639374.2014.917447.

Littletree, Sandra, Miranda Belarde-Lewis, and Marisa Duarte. "Centering Relationality: A Conceptual Model to Advance Indigenous Knowledge Organization Practices." *Knowledge Organization* 47, no. 5 (2020): 410-426. DOI: 10.5771/0943-7444-2020-5-410.

Littletree, Sandra, and Cheryl Metoyer. "Knowledge Organization from an Indigenous Perspective: The Mashantucket Pequot Thesaurus of American Indian Terminology Project." *Classification & Cataloging Quarterly* 53, no. 5-6 (2015): 640-657. DOI: 10.1080/01639374.2015.1010113.

Olson, Hope A. *The Power to Name: Locating the Limits of Subject Representation in Libraries.* Kluwer Academic Publishers, 2002.

Olson, Hope A. "How We Construct Subjects: A Feminist Analysis." *Library Trends*, 56, no. 2 (2007), 509-541. DOI:10.1353/lib.2008.0007.

Pack, Sam. *Oral History Reimagined: Emerging Research and Opportunities*. Hershey, PA: Information Science Reference, 2020.

Pritchard, Sarah M. "Developing Criteria for Database Evaluation: The Example of Women's Studies." *Reference Librarian* 4, no. 11 (1984): 247-261. DOI: 10.1300/j120v04n11_19.

Van der Wel, J. "The Realization of the Queer Thesaurus." Paper presented at the Refiguring the Archive Seminar Series, University of the Witwatersrand, South Africa. September 29, 1998.

Acknowledgments

This project, like those it documents, would not be possible without the collaboration and cooperation of many. First and foremost, we give our heartfelt thanks to each project contributor: Richard Chabrán, Lillian Castillo-Speed, K.J. Rawson, Adrian Williams, Mary Ellen Capek, and Sarah M. Pritchard. We are continuously inspired by your work, your stories, and your voices. Thank you for trusting us to share your stories and for all your time and effort to collaborate on not just the interviews, but also bringing this book to life.

The *Ways of Knowing Oral History Project* was funded in part by the Metropolitan New York Library Council's (METRO) Equity in Action Grant Program. We would like to thank METRO's Traci Mark and Mary Bakija for their administrative support throughout the project. Thanks to the project funding, we were able to work with independent audio producers who recorded the interviews locally to gather quality sound. Thanks to Noor Al-Samarrai, Sonia Chaidez, Kip Clark, Justin Hicks, Hana Crawford, and Stephen A. Poon for their tape sync skills. Thanks to NYU Libraries' Avery Fisher Center for providing a quiet recording space, with a special shout out to Scott Greenberg. Recording the oral histories was just the beginning of this project.

To ensure recording quality and preservation, we were lucky to work with other talented individuals: Thanks to Michael Cacioppo Belantara for his sound-mix mastery and incredible attention to detail in tidying up over six hours of sound recordings to make sure everyone sounded their best. We couldn't create a series of oral histories on alternative controlled vocabulary without knowing they'd be well described and findable into the future. Many thanks to Matthew Haugen for his thorough and thoughtful cataloging work. His comprehensiveness and care created exemplary catalog records. Thanks to colleagues at NYU Libraries: Shannon O'Neill for advising us on best practices regarding release and donor agreement forms, Alexandra Provo for metadata and digital library guidance, and Alex Whelan for metadata guidance and for ingesting the catalog records in collaboration with Joohwi Kim. Thanks to NYU Libraries' Digital Library Technology Services team for helping us preserve and deposit the oral histories.

The release of the oral histories in 2021 wouldn't have felt as official without a sharp looking image to communicate the project's message. Thanks to artist and musician Inaiah Lujan for his gorgeous and thoughtful project identity design. He captured the project's essence so beautifully.

We are incredibly grateful to have the chance to work with such thoughtful and helpful editors. Deep appreciation to Violet Fox and Kelsey George for your close attention to the text and thoughtful feedback.

We reserve a final word of thanks for the library workers, scholars, and activists everywhere who fight for justice in the stacks, in the catalog, at the reference desk, in the classroom, and in the world. Solidarity forever.

Index

acronym(s), 171, 172, 202
activist(s), 3, 9, 81-2, 88-9, 92n, 106, 119, 124, 127, 131-2, 134, 143-5, 146n, 147
Advanced Data Management, 112
advocacy, 147
Africana, Asian American, Chicano, & Native American Studies Center (AAACNA), 20
ALA-ACRL Women's and Gender Studies Section, 122
ALA Task Force on Women's Studies Database Evaluation, 129
algorithmic retrieval, 148
Allen, Donna, 145-6
Alpha Micro 1000, 64-6, 76
Amazons (subject term), 217
American Association of University Women (AAUW), 134
American Council on Education's National Identification Program for the Advancement of Women in Higher Education (ACENIP), 88
American Library Association (ALA), 34, 77, 82-3, 121, 128
Anderson, Steven, 174
Anna Blamanhuis (library), 155-7
anti-war movement, 17, 124

Arbery, Ahmaud, 205
Associated Students of the University of California (ASUC), 22
Association of College and Research Libraries (ACRL) Women's Studies Discussion Group, 142
Aztlán (journal), 26n, 73

Baeza, Gilda, 28
BASIC (computer language), 64, 66
Benson Latin American Collection, 43
Berman, Sanford "Sandy", 2, 33
bias, 2, 33n, 130
Bibliography of Writings on La Mujer, 40
Billey, Amber, 166-7
birth control movement, 149
Black Lesbian Archives, 164, 170
BRS (database), 29
Business and Professional Women's Foundation (BPW), 83, 89-91, 96, 107, 134, 147

Caballero, Cesar, 28
Capek, Mary Ellen, 6, 81-3, 134, 136, 138, 147

card catalog(s), 38, 127
Castillo-Speed, Lillian, 10-11, 36, 40
Castro, Rafaela, 28
catalogers, 3-4, 34, 150, 152, 212, 214, 217
cataloging, 2-3, 78, 92, 117, 125, 127-8, 137, 141-2, 150, 152, 170, 180, 186, 197, 201, 212, 216
CD-ROM, 11, 69-70, 72-3
Center for Puerto Rican Studies at Hunter College at the City University of New York, 36
Chabrán, Richard, 5, 9-11, 54, 57-8, 69
Chamberlain, Mariam, 137
Chaparro, Luis, 28
Chavarría, Elvira, 28
Chicana(s) (subject terms), 40, 67
Chicano Classification System, 10, 24, 35n, 37-8, 58-9
Chicano Database, 10-11, 50, 56, 68-73, 80
Chicano journals, 54, 57, 73
Chicano Movement, 17, 54, 73
Chicano Periodical Index, 5, 10-11, 14, 25-8, 32, 43, 56-8, 60, 69-70
Chicano periodical indexing project, 26n, 54
Chicano serials project, 26
Chicano Studies, 10, 17, 21, 26, 37, 44, 54, 60, 73-4
Chicano Studies Center Research Library (UCLA), 9-10, 54, 64, 68

Chicano Studies Library (UC-Berkeley), 9-10, 14-6, 21, 23, 35n, 41, 53, 55, 58-9, 63, 68-9, 76
Chicanos, 17, 19, 24-5, 27, 32, 45
Circumcision (subject term), 107, 112-3
Cifor, Marika, 167
civil rights movement, 17
Classification Web, 197
Clitoridectomy (subject term), 82, 113
Colbert, Jay, 167
collaboration(s), 81, 91, 98-9, 168-71, 172-3, 177, 183, 190-1
collaborators, 162, 177, 192
colonialism, 200
Committee for the Development of Subject Access to Chicano Literature, 10, 28, 34
computer technology, 56, 79
Contact dyke (subject term), 109
controlled vocabulary/ies, 1, 5, 10, 32, 55, 77, 162, 174, 214, 219
conversation(s), 35, 39, 43, 63, 69, 94, 97, 161, 164-5, 174-5, 177-8, 186, 189-91, 192, 194, 197, 203, 214-5
Corral, Norma, 31
COVID (pandemic), 80, 212-3
Cricket Press, 182
critical race theory, 176
cross references, 136, 148
cultural differences, 108, 143
cultural terms, 36, 75, 108, 200

Dewey Decimal Classification (DCC), 2, 23, 137
Dialog (databate), 29
Digital Transgender Archive (DTA), 155, 157, 161-2, 173-4, 182, 189
discoverability, 3, 5, 21-2, 41, 165, 176, 186, 204
documentation, 28, 118, 155, 177, 206, 220
Domestic violence (subject term), 82, 92, 94
DOS, 66
Drag (journal), 165
DTA *see* Digital Transgender Archive
Dukes, Earnstein, 152
Durán, Karin, 28

EBSCO, 68-71, 76
editorial board(s), 156-7, 166-8, 171, 174, 181, 191-2, 213, 215
Education Resources Information Center (ERIC), 30
El Grito (journal), 26n, 73
emic, 37
ephemera, 20, 38, 81, 91, 128, 133
ERIC Clearinghouse on Mexican Americans, 30
Ethnic Studies Library, 59-60
ethnicity terms, 177, 200-1, 214-5
etic, 37

FAMULUS (software), 30
Fantasia Fair, 165

farm workers, 18, 20, 74, 146n
female circumcision, 107, 112, 146
Feminist Dictionary, 109
feminist literature, 81
Feminist Task Force, 96n, 134
feminist terms, 82, 131, 143, 149
Fischer, Rachel, 206
Floyd, George, 204
Ford Foundation, 82, 88, 99-100, 137
Free Speech Movement, 17
free text searching, 106, 126-7, 131-2, 141, 148-9
Fresno State, 220-1
funding, 10, 43, 45-6, 58, 70, 88, 91, 99-100, 117, 133, 135, 137, 173-4, 177, 192

G.K. Hall, 31-2, 41, 55, 57, 69
García Ayvens, Francisco, 29-31, 36, 38, 44, 53-9, 63-5, 72, 74, 76
gay marriage (subject term), 170
GLBT ALMS Conference, 162
Goldstein, Janet, 111
Google, 52, 106, 126, 141, 148, 185, 190, 207, 220
Greenblatt, Ellen, 155, 157, 163
Griswold del Castillo, Richard, 17

Harper & Row, 82, 84, 108, 111-2, 115
hierarchical term(s), 39, 93, 107, 155, 157, 163, 181
hierarchy/ies, 107, 112, 164, 181
historians, 25, 128n, 131

history notes, 192
Holt, Tom, 30, 38-9, 57, 65
Homodok, 155-7, 163
Homosaurus logo, 182-3, 185

IHLIA *see* Internationaal Homo/Lesbisch Informatiescentrum en Archief (IHLIA)
Illegal aliens (subject term), 9, 24, 33-4, 40, 62-3, 132
index terms, 29, 63, 75, 82
indexes, 27, 129-31
indexing language(s), 130-3, 136, 138
Inter University Consortium for Latino Studies, 36
Inter-America Research Associates, 83, 91, 96, 102
Internationaal Homo/Lesbisch Informatiescentrum en Archief (IHLIA), 155, 157, 219
International Center for Research on Women, 86, 88
International Federation of Library Associations (IFLA), 149
intersectionality, 176, 201, 143-4, 201

Jeffries, Kristen, 75

Kazlauskas, Ed, 38
King, Pat, 82, 93, 96, 100
Kizzie, Janaya, 167
Kramarae, Cheris, 109
Kronk, Claire, 167

La Asociación de Bibliotecas Chicanas (ABC), 20, 34n
La Raza, 10, 17-8
Lakoff, George, 149
Land grants (subject term), 41
Latino studies, 23, 36, 44
LCDGT, 201-2
LD4 Conference, 204, 213, 217
League of Women Voters, 146n, 147
Lesbian (subject term), 177, 179, 218
lesbian(s), 92n, 109, 200-1, 217
  materials, 155-6
  vocabulary, 200, 219
lexicographer, 75
LGBTQ+, 155-7, 204, 206
  acronym, 172
  materials/resources, 155-7, 163, 198, 207, 220
  terms/vocabularies, 11, 40, 68, 175-7, 179, 181, 184, 186, 188, 192, 199, 201, 204-5, 211, 217-8, 220
librarian(s), 3, 10-1, 23, 28-9, 37, 43-4, 55, 57, 59, 77, 80, 82, 91-2, 96, 100, 125, 128-30, 134-9, 142, 145, 147, 152, 170, 206, 220
  as activists, 123, 125, 127
  cataloging, 212
  Chicano/Latino, 5, 35-6, 40, 54, 60
  feminist, 82
  queer, 5, 175
  reference, 31, 125-6, 132, 150, 205, 211

Library of Congress, 3-4, 11, 14, 37, 40-1, 44, 46, 77, 114, 117, 125-6, 128, 132, 135, 140, 142, 146, 150, 152, 197

Library of Congress Classification (LCC), 2, 20, 23-5, 59, 208

Library of Congress Demographic Group Terms (LCDGT), 202

Library of Congress Genre Form Terms (LCGFT), 203

Library of Congress Subject Headings (LCSH), see also subject headings, 2, 9-10, 35, 37, 43, 92, 131-2, 136-7, 144, 149-50, 155, 162, 203

Library of Congress's Subject Authority Cooperative Program, 3

linguistic(s), 21, 25, 87, 106, 119, 170, 180

linked data, 102, 156-7, 159, 174, 176, 183-4, 186, 207-8, 213, 218

Linked Data for Libraries (LD4) Conference see LD4 Conference

Literatura Chicanesca, 24, 40

looksism (subject term), 131, 143

Lorde, Audre, 100

Machine Assisted Reference Section (MARS), 130

Machine-Readable Cataloging (MARC) see MARC

Maekdo, Krü, 169, 177

MARC fields, 11, 41, 84, 74, 77, 137-8, 192

MARC records, 40, 44, 114, 117, 150-2, 198, 203, 208-9

Mariscal, Linda, 30

Marshall, Joan, 142

McCallum Sally, 77

McDowell, Robert, 28

Media Report to Women, 145-6

Medical Subject Headings (MeSH), 131n, 150

Mental Health Database, 35

metadata, 4, 127-8, 148, 163, 187, 196-7, 206-8

Microsoft Access, 76

Mikveh (subject term), 108

Milo, Albert, 28

Mobile, 99

monographic literature, 23, 130-2

Mosaic, 141

multilingual, 139-40, 149, 193

National Chicano Research Network, 29

National Council for Research on Women (NCRW), 81, 83, 88-90, 133, 134n, 135, 139, 144, 147

National Women's Studies Association (NWSA), 133, 138, 142

Native American(s), 20, 46, 109

Netherlands, 106, 142, 156, 214

New Mexico Library Association, 34

Noland, Chloe, 167

non-binary, 198, 219

Non-binary (subject term), 204, 218-9

norms, 2, 144, 188-9

Northeastern University, 156, 173

Online Computer Library Center (OCLC), 70-1, 151, 208-9
off our backs (journal), 143
online searching, 29, 130, 141, 148

pandemic *see* COVID
Parker, Barbara, 147
Polyamory (subject term), 198, 209
power, 1-2, 87, 98, 180, 215, 218
Pritchard, Sarah M., 82, 93, 96, 114
privilege, 118, 144, 180
processing manual, 29
Prostitution (subject term) *see also* Sex work, 110-1
Puerto Rican(s), 15, 36, 45, 73

qualifier(s), 149, 181
queer theory, 165, 188
Queer Thesaurus, 155-7
queer language/vocabulary, 161, 175-7, 179-80, 185, 187-9, 218-9
Quintana, Helena, 28

race, 17n, 36, 89, 96-7, 106, 108, 143-4, 169, 177, 201, 206
Racial profiling (subject term), 63
Rawson, K.J., 5, 155-7, 214
Raz, Hilda, 94
Reader's Guide, 54, 129
reference services, 127, 136
religion, 145, 218
reparative description, 3, 163
Research Libraries Group (RLG), 70-1, 76

Retter-Vargas, Yolanda, 68
revision(s), 35, 67-8, 156-7, 174, 176, 178-9, 195, 198, 214
Rich, Adrienne, 92, 95, 100
Rios, Betty Rose, 30
Rodriguez, Ron, 28
Roget's Thesaurus, 93, 108
Roles, Caitlin, 177

Sanger, Margaret, 149
Schlesinger Library, 86, 93, 96, 100, 103, 118
Science and technology (subject term), 106
scope notes, 172, 187-8, 192, 217
search engine optimization, 148
search engines, 141
Searing, Sue, 82, 93, 96, 135
Sears List, 137
see/see also, 140
self-determination, 1, 19
Semantic Web, 207, 213
Senate Concurrent Resolution 23, 43
Sex work (subject term) *see also* Prostitution, 110-1
sexism, 5, 95, 96n, 130, 144
Sexual harassment (subject term), 82, 92, 94
shelf heading list, 20, 38
Sherman, Sarah, 146
Sloan, Cheryl, 91, 96-7, 147

software, 14, 30-1, 38, 52, 67, 112, 134, 141, 174, 193
stereotypes, 110, 178
Stimson, Catherine, 117
Stineman, Esther, 135
structured searching, 141
subject analysis, 221
subject group(s), 97-8, 104, 109, 112, 114, 142-3, 147
subject headings, *see also* Library of Congress Subject Headings (LCSH), 2, 29, 32-3, 37-8, 55, 61, 101, 127, 132, 151-2, 175, 197-8, 207
syndetic structure, 136, 140-1, 155

tagging/tags, 131, 148-9, 165
Taxonomies,141
Taylor, Breonna, 204, 205n
terminology, 9, 24, 33-4, 41, 56, 107-8, 128, 130-2, 136-7, 139-40, 143-4, 148-9, 175-6, 178, 181, 185-7, 192, 207, 211
Texas Library Association, 27, 34
The Prairie Schooner (journal), 94-5
thesaurus structure, 142, 157
Third World Liberation Front, 9-10, 15n
Third World Strike, 10, 15, 22
trans communities, 163, 180, 188
trans materials, 162, 181, 198
trans people, 169, 178-80, 188, 203
trans terms, 169, 176, 179-80, 188-9, 205
Transgender (subject term), 181, 218
Transgender Tapestry (journal), 165
translation(s), 164, 184, 192, 200, 220
Trujillo, Robert, 36, 38

UN Decade for Women, 133-4, 144
uncommons, 4, 6
Undocumented children (subject term), 63
Undocumented persons (subject term), 40
Undocumented residents (subject term), 63
Undocumented workers (subject term), 40, 63
Uniform Resource Indicator (URI), 183-4, 200, 207, 209
United Farm Workers, 20
University of Kentucky, 170, 197, 203, 206, 220
use for, 67
user warrant, 216

Van der Wel, Jack, 155-7, 162, 167
Vort Corporation, 29-31, 39, 43, 57

Walker, Cat, 166
Watson, Bri, 167, 201
Whaley, Sara, 142
Williams, Adrian, 167, 170
Women (subject term), 127-8, 140, 145, 149
women's center(s), 5, 82-3, 133-5, 137, 142, 144-6, 149, 152
Women's Educational Equity Communications Network, 83, 90-1
women's history, 81, 128, 135
Women's Information Services Network, 83

Women's Review of Books, 129
women's studies, 81, 117, 123, 127-31, 134-5, 144-6
Women's Studies Abstracts, 142
Women's Studies Database Task Force, 82-3, 129
Women's Thesaurus Task Force, 82-3, 95-6
word list(s), 4-5, 41, 111, 136, 156
working group(s), 92, 191-2
worldbuilding, 3-4
worldmaking, 2, 181, 186
WorldShare Record Manager, 208-9

Yañez, Elva, 35

www.ingramcontent.com/pod-product-compliance
Lightning Source LLC
Chambersburg PA
CBHW051355290426
44108CB00015B/2026